SCHOOL ADMINISTRATOR'S STAFF DEVELOPMENT ACTIVITIES MANUAL

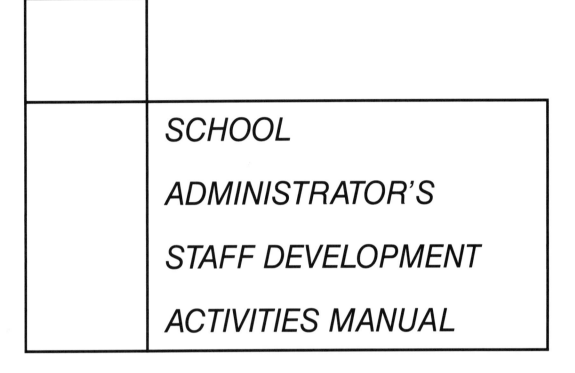

SCHOOL ADMINISTRATOR'S STAFF DEVELOPMENT ACTIVITIES MANUAL

RONALD T. HYMAN
Professor of Education
Graduate School of Education
Rutgers University

PRENTICE HALL
Englewood Cliffs, New Jersey 07632

Prentice-Hall International, Inc., *London*
Prentice-Hall of Australia, Pty. Ltd., *Sydney*
Prentice-Hall Canada, Inc., *Toronto*
Prentice-Hall of India Private Ltd., *New Delhi*
Prentice-Hall of Japan, Inc., *Tokyo*
Prentice-Hall of Southeast Asia Pte. Ltd., *Singapore*
Whitehall Books, Ltd., Wellington, *New Zealand*
Editora Prentice-Hall do Brasil Ltda., *Rio de Janeiro*
Prentice Hall Hispanoamericana, S.A., *Mexico*

© 1986 *by*

PRENTICE-HALL

Englewood Cliffs, N.J.

10   9   8   7

Dedicated, once again,
to
Suzanne, Jonathan, Elana
and Rachel

Library of Congress Cataloging-in-Publication Data

Hyman, Ronald T.
  School administrator's staff development activities
manual.

  Includes index.
  1. Teachers' workshops—Handbooks, manuals,
etc.   2. Teachers—In-service training—Handbooks, manuals,
etc.   3. Activity programs in education—Handbooks,
manuals, etc.   4. School supervision—Handbooks,
manuals, etc.   I. Title.
LB1743.H93 1986   371.1'46   85-28250

ISBN 0-13-792607-3

PRENTICE HALL
Career & Personal Development
Englewood Cliffs, NJ 07632
A Simon & Schuster Company

On the World Wide Web at http://www.phdirect.com

Printed in the United States of America

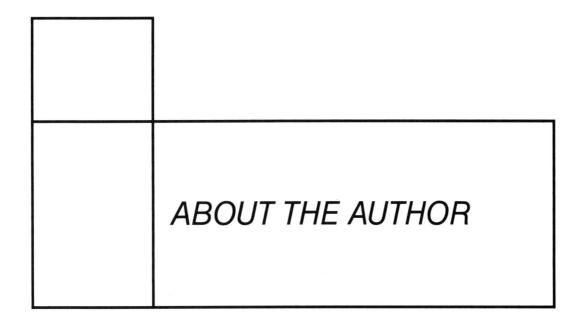

ABOUT THE AUTHOR

Ronald T. Hyman, Ed.D. (Columbia University, New York), M.A.T. (Vanderbilt University, Nashville), has been involved with education for over thirty years.

During that time, he has been a public school teacher and chairperson, research assistant, graduate school department chairperson, and college professor. In addition, Dr. Hyman has written and co-authored over twenty books, including *School Administrator's Handbook of Teacher Supervision and Evaluation Methods* (Prentice-Hall, Inc., 1975), and over fifty-five articles and reviews for such professional publications as *Educational Leadership, Journal of Teacher Education,* and *Educational Administration Quarterly.*

Dr. Hyman is presently a professor of education in the Graduate School of Education at Rutgers University (New Brunswick, New Jersey).

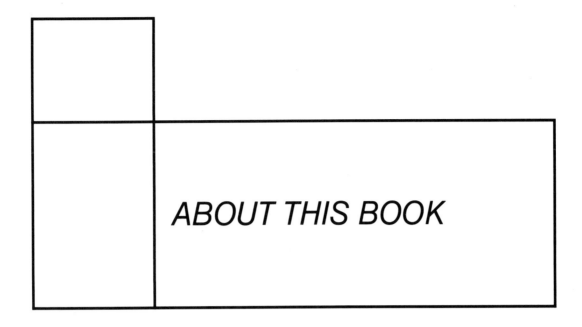

ABOUT THIS BOOK

The *School Administrator's Staff Development Activities Manual* is a practical, working tool for K–12 supervising school administrators to use in stimulating professional growth in their staffs. This book provides the means for conducting structured, thought-provoking activities during faculty meetings and other in-service workshops.

Unlike most other books on supervision that deal primarily with theory, the *Manual* gives you seven step-by-step activities that are simple to use. To help your effectiveness as a staff leader, dozens of reproducible blank forms also are included for use when conducting these activities. Because teachers are active people, you need to offer them activities to engage and challenge them, allowing all participants to raise and discuss the issues that concern and interest them.

Chapter 1 sets the stage for using the activities. It explains the functions and characteristics of a faculty meeting which, handled effectively, will enable you to lead your staff successfully through the structured activities.

Chapters 2 through 8 give you seven complete, structured activities, each concentrating on a specific set of skills:

- Colored Broken Squares (*Cooperation and Communication*)
- The Penny (*Observation, Inference, and Evaluation*)
- The Prisoner's Dilemma (*Trust and Group Benefit*)
- The Supervision Window (*Awareness and Openness*)
- Sherlock (*Collaboration and Interdependence*)
- Winter Crash Survival (*Group Decision Making*)
- The Spelling Test (*Evaluation*)

In each structured activity, a person or group performs and then discusses problem situations and solutions under the guidance of a leader. The leader directs the procedures, announces the rules, and leads the debriefing discussion so that the participants reflect on the results in an organized way.

The staff development activities foster the following types of growth and provide these benefits:

- Facilitate interaction among teachers and supervisors. Each activity encourages people to communicate with and, hence, learn from others. Peer learning, often the most effective learning technique you can offer the group, takes place, drastically reducing or removing polarization between teachers and supervisor. Furthermore, since teachers are teaching each other, they help to create a healthy supervisory atmosphere.

- Motivate the teachers and the supervisor, as the activities are enjoyable and of high interest.

- Use time effectively. In a relatively short period of time, you can work on the essential elements of good supervision.

- Offer a welcome break from the conventional approach to supervision (too often a lecture), which may be dull or threatening.

- Illustrate particular themes with noticeable and significant impact on the participants.

- Provide the teacher and supervisor with a common, unifying experience that serves as a reference point for everyone involved in teaching and supervising.

- Creat a nonthreatening situation in which everyone participates, is involved, and has fun while learning. The activities aid open discussions of key points raised by the participants themselves as they relate the activities to their own lives.

- Foster the degree of involvement that lets participants feel and observe the processes that lead to learning. Participants simultaneously learn something about themselves *and* the skill of the activity, which gives them insights that bring about change in their future behavior.

- Integrate the participants' thought processes with their concrete emotional reactions. This integration of conceptual analysis, understanding, and synthesis with personal attitudes and values helps the participants understand and label their reactions in a new way as they begin to make sense of their experiences. This, in turn, leads to change.

Read, implement, and refine these staff development activities however they best suit you and your teachers. Together, you will be taking the road to professional growth.

Note: All the activities in this manual will be useful all year long, particularly when combined with the information in the *School Administrator's Faculty Supervision Handbook,* also published by Prentice-Hall, Inc. The *Handbook* will clarify and expand the skills you need in observing, conferring, and writing reports.

Ronald T. Hyman

HOW TO USE THESE STRUCTURED ACTIVITIES

There are two aims in using the seven activities offered in this manual: to improve classroom teaching and to improve your own supervisory skills. Let's take a closer look at each one.

TO IMPROVE CLASSROOM TEACHING

You can conduct an activity as you work with a teacher or group of teachers on ways to improve their efforts in the classroom. For example, you are working with Joe Jones on his organization of class time. You find, during your observations of Joe's classroom teaching, that he almost always uses whole-group instruction, and Joe confirms this during one of your conferences. Since you recognize the advantages of employing other methods of grouping students, and because parents and students have raised this issue, you decide to help Joe bring some variety to his teaching style. To bring home your message about the advantages of small groups, you can use Sherlock, Colored Broken Squares, Winter Crash Survival, or The Spelling Test activities. Not only will you be able to make your point about the effectiveness and desirability of small groups, but you can also give Joe himself some experience working in a small group.

First, arrange the time, place, and group of individuals to be involved in the activity so Joe—and others—can benefit. Then, as you debrief, focus on the theme associated with the activity and how teachers can use small groups in their classrooms to foster learning in general. Privately suggest to Joe that he use the very same activity in his classroom, either as is or in modified form appropriate for his particular grade level.

These activities work effectively with both students and teachers in a wide range of subject areas. For example, you can use The Spelling Test not only with language arts and English teachers, but also with social studies, science, math, and arts teachers since evaluation cuts across all subject areas. Similarly, The Penny and The Prisoner's Dilemma apply to all subjects.

TO IMPROVE YOUR SUPERVISORY SKILLS

In addition to improving classroom teaching, you can also use the structured activities as you focus on supervision directly with your faculty. There are times when you must confer with teachers about how they and you can improve interaction with each other.

Suppose you find that your faculty meetings generally give you a headache because of the strife and lack of accomplishment that come with them. You could conduct Winter Crash Survival, The Supervision Window, Colored Broken Squares, or The Prisoner's Dilemma. As you debrief your staff after the activity, you can focus on the supervisory process in order to connect the theme with how the teacher and you interact to establish a particular pattern of conducting yourselves at faculty meetings. If you wish to have someone else conduct the activity because you, yourself, are too closely involved in the situation to handle it objectively, you can arrange for another person to serve as leader. The key is that the entire group be involved so people can have a positive experience and raise points that will result in improved faculty meetings.

Whichever way you use the activity, approach the training session with an attitude of open-mindedness because you can never predict exactly what will happen among the participants. You have a general idea of the outcome, but the particulars may surprise you. Each activity permits and encourages interaction among the participants, during both the action and the debriefing. New things happen at both stages each time you use the new developments rather than be thrown by them. Since each session will be unique, you won't be bored. On the contrary, your experiences will become richer and deeper as you integrate the new ideas into your daily interactions. In addition, try to create an atmosphere of openness that can yield an enjoyable and important learning experience, an opportunity to take the first steps toward the improvement of teaching and supervision.

You may find it helpful to rehearse the techniques and activities with relatives and friends. In this informal dry run, you can proceed slowly, with chapter in hand, to get the feel of the activity. You can thus debug your own approach so things will proceed smoothly when you conduct the activity with your faculty. You should be able to gather a pilot group easily, since only a group of five is needed for a trial run. In this less threatening situation, you can learn more about the activity while deciding the best way to use it with your full staff.

HOW TO READ THE STRUCTURED ACTIVITIES

The key to reading the activities is patience. Occasionally, it can be difficult to read instructions for completing a complex task with no one else to show how or answer questions about sticky points. For these reasons, you need to read slowly as you go through an activity for the first time. You may even need to reread certain early sections after some of the later ones, which may raise new questions in your mind.

It will help you to remember that you will discover more about the activity as you read, so begin with the overview. Next, read the procedural strategy for conducting the activity, and then go over the points raised by the activity. Just as you will learn more about the activity as you read, so will the participants gradually learn more as they become more involved. This process will enable them to combine cognitive learning with emotional and social involvement, to find out how the activity relates to their own lives. This is a structured yet open approach to discovery: structured in having a theme and purpose, determined by the leader, which the participants understand, and open in giving the participants the opportunity to discover the activities' meaning for themselves and their own relationships and to state them in their own way.

If you want to find out more about the activity and its relevance to your supervisory needs, skip to the points raised as soon as you have read its overview. Here you will find a list of ideas brought out by the activity, as well as a brief commentary on each. Of course, these are the ideas generally raised; your faculty may come up with new ones when using the activity. (NOTE: The points are presented *after* the procedure, so you first have an idea of how people perform the activity. This helps you appreciate the points.)

The Importance of the Procedural Strategy

Each activity has a step-by-step strategy, from introducing it, through debriefing, to launching the next session. As staff leader, you need to know this procedure so you can react to unexpected events and move smoothly to the next phase of the activity. This guidance is necessary because the interaction between leader and participant, as well as between participant and participant, is so complex.

Most of all, the activity's strategy provides a cumulative effect. When events follow a particular sequence, there is a definite, though hidden, impact because the events form a pattern that gives meaning to each particular event. It is not the specific event itself that influences us, but the context and pattern of all the events in combination. Simply stated, the strategy provides the pattern and the events cause the impact.

Why Debriefing Is Indispensable

Whenever you engage in a recreational or professional activity with a friend, colleague, or relative, you both usually talk about it afterward. This is normal, and in fact if you don't talk about it afterward, you probably feel uneasy or unsettled.

Talking about what happened during a structured activity is critical. Since participation is intended for professional development, you should not let the after-action talk drift. The structure demands that you guide the ensuing discussion.

Many experienced staff leaders claim that debriefing is the most important part of the activity, because it lends the opportunity for the participants to reflect on what they have done while discovering in their own terms the answers to: "What is this all about?" "What is the purpose of this activity?" "What did you have in mind when you brought us here for this purpose?"

The debriefing step is reflective, offering participants time to integrate the analysis of their thought processes with their group social experiences. But unless you, as leader, guide the participants to go beyond description of the action that occurred, they may get bogged down in ventilating and recounting. Participants need to move along to analyzing and seeking parallels with other aspects of their teaching lives. With your guidance, the faculty members can build on each other's comments so that the reflection that takes place is cumulative. Through the debriefing, you can lead your teachers to find meaning in the structured activity as you develop sound supervision.

A WORD ABOUT STAFF DEVELOPMENT

As staff leader, you face a dilemma. On the one hand, you know that activity and feedback are essential for learning and improvement, so you want to include these in staff development. On the other hand, you recognize that some people resist getting involved in structured activities and feedback, so you may think of skipping these steps in order to avoid group resistance.

If you take the first option, there may be unpleasantness, discomfort, and struggle because the participants resist what they feel they don't like and don't need. If you take the second option, you violate the staff development guidelines needed in helping people learn new skills. However, you do have an advantage since the participants are receiving what they feel they want and believe they need. The second option, though advantageous in the short run, has another serious disadvantage for the long run: in skipping activity and feedback, you are actually offering participants a negative example. You contradict yourself by saying with actions what you deny with words.

How is this dilemma resolved? By keeping in mind that guided activity and feedback are essential to staff development. They help your staff learn through experience and from each other.

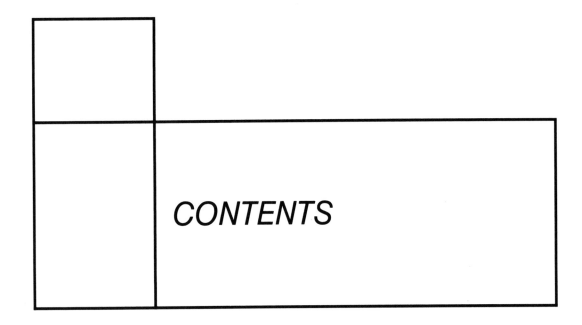

CONTENTS

1

CONDUCTING A FACULTY MEETING

Every supervisor will meet with the faculty and chair the meeting at least once during the school year. What happens at that meeting is critical to how the teachers will view you as their supervisor. Even if you have excellent relations with the faculty on a one-to-one basis, ineffective conduct as chairperson will have negative consequences for the way faculty members will subsequently behave. As chairperson, you need to continue to maintain positive relations with the faculty.

Contrary to one belief about faculty meetings, the chairperson is not solely responsible for the success of a faculty meeting. Although the chairperson does indeed conduct the meeting and lead the faculty, the responsibility for a good meeting is a joint one. The chairperson needs to be able to conduct the meeting in such a way as to demonstrate congruent leadership behavior so that the faculty continues to learn from and follow him or her. As the chairperson does this, the faculty learns that everyone is directly responsible. The knowledge, skills, and beliefs needed by you, as chairperson and supervisor, in conducting successful meetings that promote sound developmental supervision is the focus of this chapter.

After reading this chapter, you should be able to:

- Understand what constitutes a good meeting and what procedures as well as skills are needed to guide a responsible faculty.
- Distinguish between two types of faculty.
- List at least seven qualities of a good meeting for a leader-guided faculty.
- Describe four types of meetings and the considerations to be used in deciding which one to conduct.
- Know how to plan an agenda for a faculty meeting.
- List at least seven guidelines to follow in chairing a faculty meeting.
- List at least nine guidelines for effectively dealing with motions.

1

- Describe the advantages and disadvantages of voting.
- List and describe at least three alternatives to making decisions by majority vote.

WHAT MAKES A GOOD MEETING FOR YOUR FACULTY?

The question, "What makes a good meeting?" is a valid one. The answer "Good leadership" is also obviously valid. However, the problem with this answer is that it is not helpful. It does not tell you what constitutes good leadership in a faculty meeting. What should the principal or chairperson, for example, do in conducting a faculty meeting? For a complete response, you need to know answers to such questions as: Are there specific skills for conducting a meeting? If so, what are they? In what ways are the skills needed for conducting a faculty meeting different from those needed for conducting a supervisory conference? What are the types of meetings that you as a supervisor need to learn how to lead? If a good meeting is a meeting that succeeds, then what can and should you do to make a meeting succeed? To begin answering such questions in order to suggest the qualities of a good meeting, let's look at two basic types of faculty, which will set the context for the subsequent leadership skills and activities presented.

The Leader-Centered Faculty

In this type of faculty, you, the supervisor, are the focal point. You make decisions for the faculty with your power and status in mind. For example, if your faculty is considering a modification of the existing curriculum in order to integrate environmental concerns into the science and social studies programs, then you, as leader, will make decisions on:

- Membership on the curriculum committee.
- The deadline date (in order to get its approval) for presenting the committee report to the faculty and to the board of education.
- The scope of the curricular integration (that is, how much attention should be given to environmental matters relative to other matters in the science and social studies programs).
- The manner and procedure for presenting the report.

In short, through your decisions, you will assure that the faculty does what you want in order to maintain your central position as leader of the faculty. It is *your* faculty, and everyone acknowledges this.

Whether consciously or not, you will make decisions that will enhance your personal status in your school. You will get the credit for the accomplishments of your faculty committee and your faculty as a whole. You control the faculty, and the faculty serves as an extension of you in that you are the center of the staff circle with all the radii coming to and from you. To modify the metaphor slightly, you are the hub of the wheel to which the faculty spokes are connected, and without you the faculty cannot and does not function. Because you hold the faculty together, making the major and proper decisions and also providing the leadership ideas, you function as leader and representative of the faculty. You may not be consciously aware of all of this, but your actions show your purposes. Your behavior counts, and your faculty's reaction reflects your actions.

In this leader-centered faculty there is no faculty attempt to function on its own. The group knows that you have the power to make the major decisions, to implement them, and to enforce them. It may have a desire—but only a vague and weak one—to act without you. However, it realizes intuitively that it cannot do so under the current circumstances. In short, the faculty sees and currently needs you as its leader. Without you it cannot and will not function because it has learned, from its experience with you, not to function on its own. Moreover, it probably no longer knows how to function on its own since it has not developed and maintained the skills necessary to do so. From lack of practice its skill has withered away.

The Leader-Guided Faculty

In this type of faculty, you, the supervisor, function largely as the executive secretary of the faculty. You both respond to the overall policy set by the community (that is, the citizens as represented by the board of education) and guide policy through your advice and decisions. You move forward as you carry out the will of the community and also as you implement the will of the faculty as its official leader. This is true whether you are the head professional educator of the entire faculty or of a subsection of it, such as the fine arts department. You make decisions in order to carry out the will of the faculty.

However, you do not only react to or follow the faculty. You guide it; lead it; advise it; and direct it, also. You make your decisions with the progress, will, and welfare of the faculty in mind. The accomplishments and status of the faculty are central to you. Your primary concern is the promotion of the welfare of the general faculty and the students, of course, rather than your own personal status. You seek credit for the faculty because they are professionals entrusted with the education of the students. You hope and expect that the faculty will function without you when you are temporarily or permanently no longer its leader. Therefore, you take steps to develop the procedures and skills that will allow for the faculty to do so. Your leadership of the faculty is not one long "ego trip," to use a current term, for your personal gain. Rather, your focus is the continuing development of the faculty. You do not own the faculty. The faculty owns itself. You lead the faculty as well as react to it.

For example, if your faculty is considering a modification of the fine arts aspect of the curriculum, then you as leader of this leader-guided faculty will:

- Carefully differentiate between what decisions are yours alone to make as official leader and what decisions are the faculty's to make as professional educators in the school.
- Consult with the faculty before and as you make your executive decisions so that you will not be too far ahead of the faculty (so that the faculty will follow your lead and you will not lose the faculty in your consideration of where to go).
- Participate with the faculty in deciding issues of policy which belong to the faculty at large.
- Recommend specific curriculum directions to take and discuss with the faculty the implications of the various modifications suggested.

In this fine arts curriculum example, you might recommend that a modern, interpretive dance program and also a creative drama program become integral parts of your core fine arts program. This, you point out, will lead, among other things, to more school presentations by the students as well as more students in the building after class hours due to needed rehearsal time. There will probably ensue some conflict with several existing after-school programs, such as intramural sports. There may also arise conflicts with staff schedules. But the added emphasis on and expansion of the aesthetic realm of the school's life is worth it, you feel, in terms of the opportunities for the students to understand and express themselves artistically. In short, you recommend, discuss, and consult with the faculty because you see your function as guiding leader. The function of your leadership in such a faculty is to foster the participation and success of the faculty to its fullest. You lead so that the faculty can determine and accomplish its purpose.

Which Is the Preferred Type of Faculty?

The leader-guided faculty is a healthy one. Such a faculty can continue to function well when any key member leaves and even during a changeover period between leaders. Such a faculty has high morale because members recognize that the smooth functioning of the school depends on each person performing as a mature professional. This faculty is a responsible one.

In the leader-guided faculty there exists cooperation and a sense of camaraderie, both of which foster healthy interpersonal relations with and among students as the tone set by the faculty permeates the school. Conflict is accepted as normal, as a result of individuals' attempts to solve their problems. Such a leader-guided faculty, with its focus on the welfare of the group, clearly—and wisely—avoids a "personality cult" around the leader in favor of the shared mission of providing a responsible education for the students. Such a faculty seeks to develop trust among its members so that as the group works toward accomplishing its mission its individual constituents can continue to grow professionally.

It is important to keep this preference in mind because the qualities of a good meeting relate to it. The skills to be identified here—ones that you should employ in conducting a faculty meeting—are skills congruent with the leader-guided faculty. If you wish to foster a leader-centered faculty, then you will find these qualities and skills incongruous and unacceptable. If you strive to develop a leader-centered faculty, you are reading the wrong chapter, indeed the wrong book, since developmental supervision has as one of its fundamental aims the promotion of faculty initiative and responsibility. Developmental supervision fosters the advancement and refinement of faculty skills, whereas one net effect of a leader-centered faculty is the "deskilling" of the faculty regarding leadership and decision making.

Qualities of a Good Meeting

There is no precise way to identify a meeting as a good meeting as opposed to a poor or mediocre one. With regard to extreme cases, it is probably easy to get agreement among people. But once you get away from the extremes, it is always easier for people to disagree. To foster agreement and a common notion about what constitutes a good meeting, the following nine characteristics are offered.

THE MEETING ACCOMPLISHES ITS OBJECTIVES

The objectives of a meeting are set forth in the agenda. As chairperson, you know the agenda and you should present it to your faculty, preferably in writing before the meeting begins. If you haven't formally written out an agenda, then give the agenda orally to let everyone know what to expect. (If the meeting is the first convening of just a few people, for example a three-person committee meeting, you can develop an agenda with the others as your first order of business.) A good meeting is one which succeeds in accomplishing what it sets out to accomplish as set forth in the agenda. It meets the participants' expectations of what should or will occur.

THE MEETING PROVIDES NEW AND NEEDED INFORMATION

At a good meeting the participants learn further information that they need to know in order to function well in their jobs. They need this information as the meeting proceeds since it is the basis of decision making—the basis for voting on motions which are raised. They may need this information to discuss problems facing the faculty and to reach solutions. Not included in this characteristic of "new and needed information" are simple announcements and directives. If a chairperson uses meeting time merely to announce dates of future events, for example, there is no need for a faculty *meeting* since a printed announcement sheet could have been used. New and needed information is appropriate at a meeting when:

1. It is to be used in the ensuing discussion of an issue.
2. It is brief and so recent that no printed or other form of dissemination was possible.
3. It comes from someone special (for example, an outside consultant) whose very presence, delivery, and answers to questions seeking clarification are central to the new information.
4. It is part of the giver's overall purpose of convincing participants about a particular point.

Participants are rightly annoyed when they spend their precious time at a meeting hearing announcements, directives, and other information that they feel they could better learn through a memorandum in their mailboxes.

THE MEETING FOCUSES ON PROBLEM SOLVING AND DECISION MAKING

A good meeting focuses on using the participants to solve problems which face them. A good meeting goes beyond disseminating information. It encourages participants to apply the new information communicated at the meeting as they decide what action to take as a group. A good meeting involves people in something they cannot do when alone or in smaller subgroups—participate in group decision making. It encourages people to do more than vote by silently raising their "predecided" hands. It leads them to participate in discussing points publicly and then voting reasonably in consideration of the floor discussion. It fosters open communication among participants and asks them to assume "ownership" of the decisions made. A good meeting allows and encourages people to express their feelings and values on issues openly. It fosters the recognition by each person of the emotions, information, and values held by other group members as they discuss issues to be decided upon. If a meeting does not provide a forum for problem solving, a secret written ballot without any discussion is sufficient for making decisions.

THE MEETING PROMOTES A SENSE OF GROUP

A good meeting, through consideration of pertinent information and through group decision making regarding issues that affect the functions of the group, promotes an esprit de corps. A good meeting focuses on group issues and group decision making with ownership of the decisions rather than on mere apathetic physical attendance. It creates harmony and positive morale. It improves the participants' sense of devotion and loyalty to the group. It reinforces the idea that a meeting is a group endeavor. The good meeting is a time and context in which people can interact socially regarding the issues which affect them all by virtue of being in the same group.

THE MEETING FOSTERS IN THE INDIVIDUAL PARTICIPANTS A SENSE OF BELONGINGNESS

The good meeting leads individuals to contribute to the discussion of issues, the solution of problems, and the making of decisions. Through participation and interaction with others the individual senses and knows that he or she belongs to the group. The individual achieves and maintains acceptance from the group. The individual recognizes that he or she is a member of the group and has a stake in it. A good meeting incorporates potential isolates, drifters, and "attitudinal dropouts" into the group by promoting their participation and valuing their contributions.

THE MEETING ENERGIZES THE PARTICIPANTS

The good meeting leaves people with a sense of accomplishment and with a feeling of energy to work further as a group member. Though there may be at times an accompanying sense of exhaustion, a good meeting gives participants the motivation, inspiration, and reasons to pursue matters further; it fosters future willingness to work. A good meeting does not leave participants with a "recovery" syndrome such that they are demoralized and require rest and rehabilitation.

THE EXCHANGES AMONG PARTICIPANTS AT THE MEETING MANIFEST LEADERSHIP SKILLS COMPATIBLE WITH A LEADER-GUIDED FACULTY

Perhaps there is no need for this quality to be stated explicitly. Perhaps you might argue that if the first six qualities are present, then this seventh one is automatically present. Nevertheless, this quality is so important for the supervisor who conducts a meeting that it deserves separate attention. A good meeting develops because of the leadership skills performed by the meeting chairperson. A good meeting does not just occur even if relevant, fiery issues are on the agenda. The chairperson must exert positive leadership for a good meeting to occur. Through the skills manifested when, for example, introducing issues, calling on people to contribute, and contributing personally, the leader shapes a meeting consistent with a leader-guided faculty.

The good meeting results from the combined skills of the leader and the contributions of the participants. If the leader exerts autocratic control of the meeting, then the meeting cannot have the first six qualities and cannot be considered a good one. The manifested leadership skills and the preferred type of faculty must be congruent in order to have a good meeting. You can't have a good meeting without congruence.

THE MEETING ENCOURAGES FULL, FAIR, AND OPEN DISCUSSION OF ISSUES

This characteristic is obviously related to those above. Indeed, you could say that without full, fair, and open discussion it would be impossible to promote a sense of group or belongingness or to solve problems or to energize participants. Yet this item deserves separate mention because it highlights an essential aspect of our democratic life. We must act democratically if we wish to promote the furtherance of an ideal we believe in strongly. We must protect the rights of people with a minority point of view so that we do not have a "tyranny of the majority" as we allow the majority viewpoint to prevail and bind us by motions passed at the meeting. Full, fair, and open discussion of issues implies a sense of order, too, and that is part of the last characteristic since it relates to management of the meeting.

THE MEETING IS ORDERLY AND KEEPS TO ITS TIME SCHEDULE

This last point needs little embellishment. Without a sense of order no one can conduct or participate in a fruitful meeting. Without an effort to start on time and to finish on time people are frustrated in the expectations and plans for other activities in their lives. You show respect for people by how you treat them, and one aspect of this relates to your use of their time.

WHAT TYPE OF MEETING SHOULD YOU HOLD?

Every group convenes as a group at one time or another. The school faculty is no exception. Supervisors and teachers must decide how they will spend the time they devote to faculty meetings. Supervisors, because of their leadership role, most often make that decision for their individual faculty groups. Though they make this decision, most are not consciously aware of doing so because they generally follow the tradition of doing what everyone else does. Nevertheless, by planning for and conducting the meetings as they do, the supervisors make decisions even though they do not do so explicitly. Naturally, it is much better for you to be aware of what decisions you are making. By being aware, you can guard against a possible slip of acting incongruently.

The Business Meeting

There are several pure types of meetings that rarely occur in reality. Although most meetings are hybrids, let's consider the pure types first. One type of meeting is the business meeting where various leaders and committees report on their activities. (A committee may be composed of one or more persons designated to be in charge of a particular area of faculty concern.) The committees report and may even request faculty agreement or support for decisions needed by the committees in order to continue their work. For example, the committee on student activities may report on the plans for the seventh-grade class trip to Washington, D.C. The committee may then seek the faculty's approval that the trip be three days, rather than two days like last year, because the extra day will permit students to see a new exhibit at the Smithsonian Institution devoted to experiments in teaching animals to understand and imitate human speech. Similarly, the recreation committee may report on intramural basketball for the season.

In such a business meeting, the committees bring to the faculty their recommendations for faculty action and at the same time receive from the faculty its ideas on the committees' projects. The exchange between the committee and the faculty promotes a sense of group cohesion, common purpose, and clarity about the faculty's position on given activities. Though a series of committee reports during a meeting often appears boring, the function of such reports in promoting a sense of faculty responsibility and involvement is not to be dismissed or treated lightly at all.

The Policy Meeting

A second pure type is the policy meeting. Here the meeting focuses on discussing one or two major issues which set overall policy for the school or department as a whole. The policies, once determined, will provide the umbrella under which the faculty individually and in groups will conduct their affairs. It may be that the issue is raised by way of a committee report, but the focus of the meeting is the deciding of policy. Since the issue is a major one with many ramifications, the entire meeting, with the exception of one or two brief last-minute announcements, is devoted to the policy issue. Everyone realizes that the issue at hand will receive maximum time for consideration without distractions or pressure to move on to other concerns.

For example, suppose you are principal of a middle school. You are in close contact with the two faculty members who constitute your committee on student activities. Because you recognize that the request for a three-day trip to Washington, D.C., by the seventh graders will evoke much discussion about the purpose and value of class trips in general, you do not place other items on the agenda. You believe that the issue of class trips, as they conflict with teacher demands for more classroom teaching time in order to meet the pressure for improvement in fundamental skill areas, is one that deserves the faculty's careful attention. The issue is a general one and the particular trip to Washington, D.C., is but one case that needs to be decided in light of some guiding policy, which the faculty must explore in depth. Hence, you recognize that the committee's report is only the springboard for getting at the overall issue so that together the faculty can set a policy to guide further planning of activities and teaching in your school. You do not place any other items of concern on the agenda, thus conveying an important message to everyone: this issue is significant; we need a policy decision on it; we will devote all of our meeting time to it; give your undivided attention to it.

The Problem-Solving Meeting

A third pure type is the problem-solving meeting. With this type the focus is on one or two related problems that have arisen or are projected to arise and need the attention of the faculty as a group. A planning meeting is one kind of problem-solving meeting. A planning meeting deals with a projected problem or, better yet, with the prevention of a future problem. Meetings dealing with solving current problems, or solving future problems, or planning for the prevention of future problems are all similar enough for our purposes to be labeled as problem-solving meetings.

One major reason for solving the problem with the entire group is the opportunity to pool resources, experiences, and perspectives in proposing solutions as well as in examining probable consequences of each proposed solution. The solution of the group will probably be a richer one, that is, it will take into account a greater range of possibilities and consequences than a solution offered only by you as a leader. A second major reason for a problem-solving meeting is the need to involve the group in arriving at a solution so that the members will have a stake in implementing the decision. The faculty is more likely to implement a solution (even if it is the same one you thought of on your own) if it participates in proposing various solutions and investigates the pros and cons of each than if it merely receives a prepackaged solution. When the faculty is personally aware of the thinking that has gone into a solution, it is more accepting of that solution. Participation in the process is vital to the effective implementation of the solution itself.

For example, suppose you and your faculty are facing the problem of incorporating the use of personal computers into your science program for students ages twelve to eighteen (roughly middle school through high school). The problem has many aspects, two important ones of which are the history of not utilizing personal computers and the limited number of eight available computers for 1550 students. The faculty estimates that the number of computers needed is in the range of thirty-five to forty-five. Since the solution will bear on scheduling as well as on teaching, you need the ideas and cooperation of your science faculty first and foremost. You therefore raise the issue with them, seeking possible solutions before eliciting agreement on a solution that you will present to the entire faculty for approval.

The Debriefing/Implications Meeting

A fourth type of pure meeting is the debriefing/implications meeting. In this type the focus is on clarifying and understanding a major event which has directly affected the faculty. Obviously, no major event (such as last night's open board of education meeting where the superintendent unveiled plans to close a neighboring elementary school) strikes all people the same. Major events are by nature complex and deserve intense, cooperative analysis in order to understand their many ramifications. One person cannot possibly know all the details surrounding a school closing nor can any one person analyze the interconnections of the consequences and what they imply for your faculty.

For example, suppose that your school system held an in-service program devoted to the topic of family life education, which the state board of education mandated for inclusion in the curriculum for every student. The faculty attended a common lecture by the deputy state superintendent of schools and then a series of small workshops dealing with subject-matter interest and age of students taught. In light of your recognition of the significance and complexity of the topic and the in-service program, you decide to devote your faculty meeting to debriefing the day's in-service program. The reflection on the points raised by the deputy state superintendent plus the reports from the various workshops attended, as a way of sharing viewpoints, will lead you to a discussion of implications for your faculty. By devoting an entire meeting to debriefing and analyzing implications, you communicate your recognition of the seriousness of the issue.

Considerations in Deciding on the Type of Meeting

With these four pure types of meetings in mind—business, policy, problem solving, debriefing/implications—it is possible to make a more informed decision about what type of faculty meeting to hold. Surely you can decide to hold a pure debriefing/implications meeting and thereby demonstrate to your faculty—whether it be a departmental faculty or an entire school faculty—that teachers can meet together in nonroutine ways. In deciding which type of meeting to hold, you need to consider the following questions:

WHOSE DECISION IS IT?

Most likely, as leader of your faculty you have the authority to make the decision about the type of meeting. Indeed, a leader exerts leadership and guides the group by the very decisions made concerning group matters, and one important group matter is the interaction at meetings. Nevertheless, even though you may decide unilaterally, you will be wise to consult with your faculty on what the agenda should be. From your own assessment of faculty affairs, in addition to what your faculty suggests, you can make a decision that is congruent with a leader-guided faculty.

WHAT IS THE MOOD OF THE FACULTY?

You must be able to "read" the faculty in order to understand how you can best lead them. If the mood of the faculty shows confusion because there is no definite policy to guide their actions, the teachers will definitely resent a regular business meeting rather than an opportunity to speak out on issues that set guidelines for daily activities. If the faculty feels numb from hearing long-winded committee reports, it probably is pointless to hold yet another business meeting; a problem-solving meeting would probably be refreshing for them.

WHAT MAJOR ISSUES FACE THE FACULTY?

If there are major questions in education (for example, Is computer literacy basic for all students like the three R's are?) or if there are major questions in your particular school (for example, How should we prepare for a sharply decreased enrollment beginning in two years?), you must consider using faculty meetings to explore them. You may consider devoting a series of meetings to a given issue in conjunction with a half- or full-day in-service meeting.

WHAT IS YOUR CONCEPT OF A FACULTY MEETING?

If you believe that a faculty meeting must offer you the opportunity, for example, to make announcements and exhort the faculty regarding promptness in filing reports, then it is virtually impossible for you to hold policy, problem-solving, or debriefing/implications meetings. You are virtually stuck with conducting routine business meetings. However, if you believe that faculty should participate in deciding fundamental issues affecting them, you will arrange time in faculty meetings for discussions of policy, for example, and seek alternate ways to deal with promptness in filing reports. Indeed, treating the faculty as decision makers may be one way of convincing them of their stake in school matters, and hence this may decrease the need for you to exhort people about promptness in filing reports.

HOW MUCH TIME IS AVAILABLE FOR YOUR MEETING?

To begin a policy discussion on field trips when you know there is disagreement among the faculty but when you have only thirty minutes available to you is foolish. It is foolish because the chances of establishing a policy within such a short period of time are very slim. The pressure to finish within a half hour will work against careful and rational inspection of the issues involved with field trips. On the other hand, to set forth the issue and to establish procedure for fully treating the issue of field trips is possible and sensible. In short, you must consider how much time is available to you as you plan which type of meeting to hold, even if the meeting is a hybrid with elements of several pure types.

PREPARING THE AGENDA

One crucial key for fostering the qualities of a good meeting identified earlier is the well-planned agenda. The agenda gives you in outline form your plan for the meeting regarding the order of items and the time allocated for each. Without an explicit agenda, a faculty meeting has excellent chances for going astray or creating chaos in the minds of the participants. With an agenda that is known not only by you but by the participants, the meeting can proceed in an orderly way to accomplish its purposes. This is especially true in a large meeting where people with personal issues may easily overlook commonly shared issues.

Needs and Relevance

As leader, you must prepare the agenda in consideration of needs of the faculty *and* relevance. You must plan the agenda on behalf of the faculty, doing so by assessing their needs. But assessment of faculty needs is not enough for planning the agenda. Indeed, the faculty may need to establish a policy on field trips. Nevertheless, the group may not be ready or willing to establish such a policy at a meeting following the superintendent's announcement that effective this new school year the budget for printed textbooks will be decreased 50 percent in order to increase the budget for computer-related study aids.

Therefore, needs alone will not suffice since you must consider pertinence also as a criterion.

Time

Time is another factor because we all live with time constraints. A faculty meeting offers you no escape from these constraints, so you might as well accept their presence and plan with them in mind. If you have allotted to you—by union contract, school schedule, tradition, or whatever—only forty-five minutes, then you simply must accept this constraint and plan for full use of your time. Do not plan to go over the time limit. Nothing is more aggravating to faculty members than a meeting that drags on over the allotted time. Those who do not leave after forty-five minutes, for example, will be angry and resentful. Teachers must work within short time periods all day, and expect that you will do so, too. Just as students resent being kept after class by a teacher, so do teachers resent being kept afterwards by a faculty leader.

In light of the time constraints and your assessment of the needs of the faculty and what is pertinent to them, you should decide what type of meeting to hold. Perhaps the best way of doing this is to jot down on scratch paper all the items that come to mind that deserve and require faculty attention. Then review these, giving some weight of importance to each item. Consider also if you can deal with some items by memorandum (for example, choice of fish, meat, or vegetarian at the autumn dinner preceding Parents Back-to-School Night). The remaining items will lead you to a tough decision: to have a hybrid meeting devoted to several items (for example, announcements, policy on detention, and organization of graduation ceremonies), or to have a pure meeting devoted to a single complex issue (for example, solving the problem of decreasing in-school study time and space), or to have a pure type devoted to several relatively simple issues (for example, policies on scheduling of homework assignments, hall traffic, and use of videotaping and playback equipment).

There is no formula to follow in making a decision as to the type of meeting to hold. You may have to postpone some items to a future meeting and deal with others in an alternative way. You may now feel that your faculty does not respond well to memos and that it is just easier or more effective to get responses at a faculty meeting since it takes only two or three minutes to do so. However, you may find that such small items can consume up to one-third or one-half of your meeting time as well as serve as distractors of the faculty. That is, after dealing with some small issues that might have been dealt with alternatively, the faculty may be unsettled, annoyed, distracted, and unwilling to focus on the main item of the agenda.

You may have to *teach* your faculty by explicit statement and your behavior that your use of alternative means of dealing with small matters is necessary to their own continued professional behavior. It may take a while for your faculty to recognize and appreciate your stance regarding the use of time devoted to faculty meetings but the long-run pursuit of using faculty time well is worth it. They will learn and it will help you set a better tone for future faculty meetings.

Writing and Distributing the Agenda

Be realistic and write out your agenda. When you read it you will get another chance to estimate the time needed by the faculty to cope with each item. At least for yourself, put in the approximate time you will allot to each item. If there is but one item for a forty-five-minute meeting, then write in the timing for some subpoints. (See "Features of the Agenda.") Take care not to detract from the main items by scheduling many and all announcements at the opening of the meeting. A direct approach to the main and serious issues will help set a positive, professional tone. If at all possible, try to distribute a printed agenda to each person so that everyone will be aware of what is expected and the timing you project as adequate. Faculty will respect the agenda and unconsciously adjust their behavior to permit the orderly progress of the meeting as you have planned it. In short, the printed and distributed agenda is a strong device to communicate to everyone present your intentions and judgments about the value of specific items before the faculty.

Features of the Agenda

Several features of a planned agenda (see Figure 1-1) deserve your attention.

- The *length* of the meeting is specified to give advance notice to everyone of what is expected; no one should expect to leave before one hour.

- The individual items have an *estimated amount* of time allocated to them. The allocation indicates relative importance and the intention to deal with all items. This is especially important for Items 3a and 3b in order to indicate that one-half of the entire meeting is to be devoted to the main issue.

- For items which are essentially *passive*, the reports and announcements of Items 1, 2, and 3a, just the *topic listing* suffices to introduce them.

- For the item which requires more than listening—it *requires discussing and deciding*—there is a *specific question* to indicate just what the issue is. The question in Item 3b gives direction to the faculty. It contrasts with "Use of computer," which is the general topic but which by being vague doesn't direct the thinking of the faculty as they prepare themselves for that part of the agenda.

Lincoln Elementary School
Agenda—Faculty Meeting
September 14 in Multipurpose Room
2:45–3:45 p.m.

2:45–2:50	1. Last-minute announcements (Carl Voorhees)
2:50–3:10	2. Summer curriculum reports
	a. Social Studies (Kathy Jones)
	b. Language Arts (Sean Kelly)
	c. Reading (Judy Singer)
3:10–3:45	3. Use of computer: Phase I of Lincoln's program
(5 minutes)	a. Status report on new computer (Carl Voorhees)
(30 minutes)	b. How shall we provide for valuable and smooth instructional use of the computer? (Initial proposal by ad hoc computer committee; Steve Davies for the committee)

FIGURE 1-1. A planned agenda.

- The *name of the person responsible* for the agenda item is listed. This will aid in the flow of the meeting and also indicate who should be contacted for last-minute points to be raised.
- The issue which *requires faculty action*—a problem-solving or policy-issue decision—will begin with a *prepared proposal*. Here the proposal is by an ad hoc committee. Though Davies is responsible for presenting the proposal it is clear that the proposal was not drawn up by Davies alone. (See the following section for guidelines in conducting the section of the meeting dealing with a problem-solving discussion or policy issue.) This clearly indicates that the meeting will not deal with the question of computers from scratch. Rather it will start by utilizing the preliminary thinking and efforts of a committee.
- Though it is not evident from Figure 1-1, it is *preferable to distribute* the agenda in the faculty mailboxes the day before the meeting or *early in the day* of the meeting rather than at the beginning of the meeting. By knowing the agenda items before the meeting begins, the faculty can mentally prepare themselves for the meeting; they can contact people responsible for agenda items to offer additional information. If it is not possible to distribute the agenda before the meeting, then agendas should be available to people as they enter the meeting room.

It is important that, having decided upon the agenda items, you inform the person responsible for each item even before you make final decisions as to their order in the agenda and amount of time to be spent on each. Faculty members seldom, if ever, want to be called on to give a report or to offer a proposal without preparing for doing so. While a person may be able to give a five-minute report extemporaneously, though he or she may not like doing so and though it may be a bit rambling, there is little chance that a person can present a sensible, coherent proposal on a policy or problem issue without careful preparation. For the sense of coherence, it is necessary for you to contact and notify faculty members that you expect them to be responsible for a given item on the agenda.

GENERAL GUIDELINES FOR CHAIRING THE MEETING

Formal and Informal Meetings

There are essentially two types of meeting—the formal and the informal—and in practice generally they are related to size. A large faculty of seventy-five people or more will most often have formal meetings, especially if it is a school-wide meeting. Generally, a department faculty of ten to twenty has an informal meeting because people are quite familiar with each other and formal meetings are stiff and uncomfortable. A formal meeting may operate according to some set of agreed-upon rules, such as those set forth in *Robert's Rules of Order*, surely the best known set of meeting rules available to organizations. The formal meeting, especially one run by an official set of rules, allows you to conduct an orderly meeting for any size faculty group—25, 75, 125, or even 525. As with any group of people, whether it consists of teachers, students, or members of Congress, as the group increases in size the need for implementing formal rules also increases. (A parallel with teaching: You might feel comfortable lecturing formally to 100 students but you probably could not lecture to only five students whom you know personally.)

However, a group of thirty teachers constituting the entire faculty of an elementary school or small middle school need not necessarily hold strictly formal meetings. Nor must the meeting follow a specific set of rules, such as *Robert's Rules of Order* or *Sturgis Standard Code of Parliamentary Procedure*. You need not do so for two reasons:

- Your faculty most likely does not have a written constitution specifying that meetings be conducted according to a set of parliamentary rules.
- Such sets of rules are for deliberative assemblies (that is, legislative groups).

Your faculty may not constitute a large deliberative assembly needing strict, formal procedures as a way of maintaining law and order partly because you all work together daily and know each other. As leader and chairperson of your faculty meetings, you should strive to foster an easy, congenial flow of interaction among people. This is so even if the meetings are what some people would call large, but especially if they are small departmental meetings or relatively small school-wide meetings.

Furthermore, a set of meeting rules is really only a compendium of parliamentary rules (indeed, the member of an organization who is the authority on procedure is called "parliamentarian") and is intended for impersonal deliberative assemblies that must act by strict legal procedures. As one writer on organization says in reference to such sets of rules, "But in small groups, the ponderous procedures involved stymie human interaction and the flow of creativity. The rules stimulate a legalistic and mechanical way of thinking."[1] Professor King Broadrick, a lawyer and parliamentarian, in cautioning us on a strict application of an official set of rules claims that such use of rules is "likely to be nonproductive if not actually disruptive....The hazard of literal and legalistic interpretation is that it will tend to make procedure more prominent and thus more important than the substantive issues under discussion."[2]

In short, be cautious in relying on and strictly applying a set of parliamentary rules with your faculty.

An informal—or less than formal—meeting allows you more leeway in conducting your meeting. With an informal meeting, you can promote closer, more cooperative relations among members. You can also avoid entanglements with points of order, points of information, a specified order of agenda items, and other devices that some people invoke, consciously or unconsciously, to impede the progress of a meeting. An informal meeting allows you to fit your agenda to your situation. Besides, it is natural with a small group of people who know each other well to use an informal approach. Some faculties—school or department—consider themselves as "family," and it is impossible to conceive of a family using a formal procedure for deciding how to spend its vacation time.

Guidelines for the Chairperson

Much of what follows will not strike you as new. Yet, it needs to be stated explicitly because so many people still do not implement the guidelines discussed here. These guidelines tie in with the qualities of a good faculty meeting presented earlier and the actions to take in dealing with motions which are presented in the next section. By following these guidelines, *you show that you value faculty time and your own time and that faculty meetings are serious and important.*

- Begin and end on time.
- Prepare an agenda, distribute it, and stick with it by moving along according to your time estimates for each item.
- Keep on target in regard to both substantive or procedural matters; don't wander.
- Arrange for a comfortable physical environment (that is, adequate heating or cooling, good lighting, good seating, minimum noise distraction, and the like).
- Arrange for a "recorder" or "secretary-of-the-day" to provide a summary and sense of the meeting in written form.
- Arrange for coffee, tea, or cocoa and cookies or some other refreshment snack as one way of creating a warm and friendly atmosphere.
- Provide a chalkboard or overhead projector or large easel pad in order to have a large public visual display of data or motions.
- Distribute handouts as needed when in a small group, but with a large group distribute handouts before or as the meeting starts. By distributing materials at the start of the meeting with a large group, you can prevent distraction from the meeting, loss of time, and several moments of chaos as papers are passed around and read by the members.
- Suit the style of the meeting to your faculty without worrying about what parliamentary rule books recommend regarding rules and order of business for a strictly official deliberative assembly. In order to do this, you will need to know basic parliamentary procedure. A quick trip to your library will help you brush up on the fundamentals. It will be well worth your time to review the basics so you can judge how to modify formal procedure to suit your faculty.
- View the meeting as one more opportunity for you as leader to help your faculty develop further as a leader-guided faculty. Let your positive concept of the meeting guide your behavior during the meeting for the benefit of your faculty.

DEALING WITH MOTIONS

Motions are the lifeblood of a faculty meeting because it is through them that a faculty acts. A motion is a proposal for action, and an approved motion commits the faculty to act in a certain way. Motions constitute potential actions of the faculty. It is for this reason that the right to vote on motions—that is, the right to help determine what action the faculty shall take—is a highly valued right in any faculty or organization. And the rights to *propose* motions and to *discuss* motions in order to influence how colleagues will act regarding a motion on the floor are similarly prized by all.

Because motions are so crucial for a successful faculty meeting it is important for you to know how to deal with them effectively. Motions are the most important element for you to deal with well, much more so than reports and announcements. There are some guidelines for you to follow as you deal with motions whether you conduct a formal meeting run strictly according to a set of rules or an informal meeting in which you actually relax the strict parliamentary rules in order to suit the total situation and goals of your faculty. The guidelines below refer to *main motions—those motions which propose primary faculty action, require discussion and decision, and are on the floor independently.*

Be Prepared

Nothing will be as embarrassing to you personally and as destructive to the faculty generally as a motion for action by your faculty for which you are unprepared. You should have a good sense of the agenda and the members to know what will probably arise. If you are advocating a particular motion or backing a motion to be made by one of your members, you should make sure that you know the rationale supporting the motion and the principal facts connected to it. Do not wing it! If you treat a motion lightly, you risk the defeat of your motion, and then your leadership of the group will falter. This is not to say that every vote must go your way. Rather, if you lose a vote, you should lose on the merits of the issue and not because you are unprepared with a sound argument consisting of pertinent facts and explanations.

Talk with your committee chairpeople before they make a motion so you can deal with it from strength by helping possibly to modify it or rephrase it. Most of all you should understand thoroughly every motion, your own and those of others, so you can lead the discussion of it effectively. "Be prepared," though a common guideline, is crucial for motions for they constitute the actions your faculty will take and thus are a public manifestation of the leadership you are providing to your faculty.

Follow Correct Procedural Steps

If you are using motions to establish the action to be taken by your faculty no matter how informal other aspects of your meeting are, you should follow correct meeting procedure, modified slightly to suit your group, of course. (In a small group of ten or less you may choose not to use motions at all. See later in this chapter for a further comment on using consensus rather than motions.) Correct procedure will help you to have a fair and open discussion.

1. *Recognize the member* who wishes to speak.
2. Speaker *states motion*: "I move that…" ("I move that…" is preferable to "I make a motion that…" although the latter is certainly used and understood. It is also preferable to "so moved" after the chair or another person speaks about an issue such as adjournment.)
3. Another member *seconds* the motion.
4. *Restate* the motion.
5. *Call for discussion* of the motion.
6. *Restate* the motion when discussion ends.
7. *Call for a vote*: either a *voice* vote (aye and no), or a *show of hands* vote, or a *standing* vote, or a *roll call* vote, or a *secret paper ballot* vote.
8. *Announce the result* of the vote; announce that the motion is "carried" (passed) or "lost" (defeated) or give the exact count in favor and opposed whenever the specific number has been taken.

Keep in mind the general rule of thumb about a tie vote: a tie vote defeats the motion, but, as chair, you can vote in order to break the tie if you wish. (As a member of the group you can always vote although many people do not vote except to break a tie when they serve as chairperson.)

State the Motion Concisely and Affirmatively

A concise motion makes clear what the action of the faculty will be if the motion carries. If you state or help state the motion succinctly, you will avoid misinterpretation. Delete parenthetical ideas and reasons and facts supporting the motion. These items may be relevant, but they do not describe the action under consideration. They only support the action. Zero in on the action and make every effort to state the action in the positive so as to avoid confusion. Negative motions confuse the voting because a yes vote then actually opposes action. People are accustomed to voting yes to get something done, not the other way around. If need be, help the motion-maker to restate the motion succinctly and affirmatively before the discussion begins in order to encourage a meaningful discussion on the substance of the motion rather than on its semantics.

Call on the Motion-Maker to Start the Discussion

The discussion begins officially after a motion has been made, seconded, and restated by you as chairperson. To start a discussion, announce that the motion is now open for discussion. You should call on the maker of the motion to state facts and reasons for asking the group to approve the motion. (Occasionally a person makes a motion and actually wants to defeat the motion. For example, your faculty has been asked by another faculty to approve a resolution censuring the State Superintendent of Schools. In order to make it a matter of public record, a faculty person may so move but seek defeat of the motion.)

A discussion actually begins with and subsequently focuses on the facts and reasons given by the maker of the motion. There are two ways for this to occur: (1) the motion-maker gives a prelude to the motion, stating facts and reasons, and then states the motion; and (2) the motion-maker states a motion (or takes a previous meeting's motion from the table) and afterwards states the facts and reason. Rarely does a person move a motion without giving any facts or reasons, but it is a possibility. Generally, in order to secure the attention of the group, it is advisable to offer facts and reasons before stating the motion. This tactic keeps the group attentive as you build up to the motion.

Suppose a member uses the preferred approach, giving a prelude of support for the motion before actually moving the motion. Suppose this occurs as part of a committee report. After hearing (1) the report, as prelude, and then (2) the actual motion, you should (3) restate the motion, (4) announce that the motion is open for discussion, and (5) request speakers to address themselves to the facts and reasons offered by the motion-maker that you should *outline or highlight briefly*. Or you can (6) request the motion-maker to *outline or highlight briefly* two or three basic facts and reasons before you recognize other members to speak.

If, for some reason, the member moves the motion before supporting it, then (1) restate the motion, (2) have it seconded, and (3) call on the motion-maker to speak first in support of the motion. Suppose that after moving that the faculty integrate computer teaching next semester, the motion-maker says, "I support the motion to begin the use of computers as of this spring term because by then we will be settled in with our new faculty and will all have had our in-service workshop on the use of BASIC, and also because the pressure from the parents is mounting every day. I think it's time we act." At this point, other members can discuss the assertions made by the motion-maker. Now, the discussion can begin because there are facts and reasons offered just as when a motion follows a detailed report.

Focus the Discussion

Though the motion is open for discussion, faculty members should not and need not ramble on about irrelevancies or tangential matters. Focus forthcoming speakers with a *brief sentence or two* as to the main issue before them. Request that they add relevant information or other reasons—pro or con—that will help the group members to decide how to vote. In general, ask people to speak directly on the motion to help them not to wander. Faculty members, when they wander, do not intend to do so. They do so because of their interest in several matters simultaneously. By focusing the discussion you are helping people to have a more fruitful meeting.

The key in focusing is not to be too overbearing, too restrictive, or too directive so that people feel that their freedom is lost. It is a delicate balance, to be sure, between (1) focusing the discussion and (2) allowing members to speak as they see fit so they can develop their positions according to their own particular style. Nevertheless, it is important to offer some guidance and reminder that the motion on the floor deserves specific attention. After the discussion begins you can say something like, "Please comment on the reasons given or offer other facts and reasons—for or against this motion, as you prefer, but speak directly on the motion, please."

Solicit Additional Pertinent Facts and Reasons

As you listen carefully to speakers on the motion, you will notice that certain facts and reasons are given. Since you want an *open* discussion, not a railroaded discussion, you should request any further pertinent information. Do so in recognition that the faculty should decide on the basis of the good reasons given during the discussion. If not, then there is no purpose in the discussion and hence no need for the meeting—you could conduct a vote by written ballot distributed in everyone's mailbox. For example,

> YOU (as chairperson): Thanks for your comments. Are there any further facts and reasons we should know to help us decide on the motion? Just major ones now, please.

With this quick solicitation, you accomplish several things. You let your faculty know that they have the right to speak, that you do not intend to push for a hasty decision, that the decision should be based on the relevant facts and reasons (that is the essence of any discussion), and that you want only important ones at this point in the discussion probably since your allotted time is ending.

Elicit a Minority View, if Necessary

Suppose that after the mover speaks, the next two or three speakers rise to give their support to the motion. Rather than continuing to call on those people who raise their hands, you should explicitly ask for any opposing views.

> YOU (as chairperson): We've heard three people support the motion. Is there anyone who wants to speak now in opposition?

By directly calling for an opposing viewpoint, you may encourage someone who has been reluctant or shy. Your request makes it legitimate to speak out against the motion. You may find, however, that there is no strong opposition or, at least, that no one wants to offer opposing facts and reasons. But this is another matter. Thus, in essence, by offering time for opposition and finding none you may reach the point of deciding sooner. There may be no need for continued discussion on the motion because everyone agrees already. Protect the minority and encourage it to be heard.

Limit Speakers in Number and Time, if Necessary

At times you have a difficult leadership decision to make: either you limit the number of speakers on a motion and the amount of time each person can speak in order to progress through your agenda in a timely manner or you allow faculty members the right to speak and deliberate on an issue until they are satisfied that they have thoroughly discussed the points to make them ready for deciding. It is not easy to choose between the two alternatives. On the one hand, you can suggest and announce that only two or three more people will speak and that each will have only two minutes. After several additional, short faculty comments, you can call for a vote or some other way of deciding the motion. Such an approach has the distinct advantage of keeping the meeting going according to your time schedule. Besides, people may agree with you that additional speakers and time are not actually fruitful.

Yet, on the other hand, the limitation of number of speakers and the limitation of each speaker's time to speak often breeds resentment on the part of some faculty members who may believe that you are biased and maneuvering for a decision that you personally advocate. If you simply limit speakers in order to remain on a time schedule, you may achieve your time objective but at the price of a thorough discussion. Your original estimate of time may be too low, the faculty interest may be significantly keener than you predicted, and the faculty may see many more subissues in this complex issue than you do. Therefore, trying to finish with an agenda item in twenty-five minutes, for example, may be unwise, to say the least, if you care about the feelings and preferences of your faculty. You may need a special meeting just to deal with this agenda item fully.

To make a decision, you must weigh several factors within a short time. Among these are faculty interest; significance of issue; significance of other agenda items; and possible additional meeting time for completion of unfinished agenda. The guideline to help you decide in this matter is: *If you sense resistance when you begin to limit the speakers, explain the situation briefly and then quickly ask the group its preference: limit discussion and stay on schedule, or lengthen the meeting somewhat (ten to fifteen minutes, perhaps), or schedule another meeting devoted wholly to a full discussion of this issue*. Make this procedural interlude *very brief* so that you do not spend precious meeting time talking about meeting time instead of the issues at hand.

Maintain Order

Once the discussion gets underway, some people, because they are concerned with the motion, will begin to talk with their neighbors. Though the motivation for such talk is positive, you should try to keep such side talk to a minimum since it distracts the group and you from concentrating on the main discussion. Gesture and softly—but explicitly and noticeably if necessary—remind members to attend to the speaker who has the floor. Also, as people raise their hands to speak on the motion, jot their names on a list so that each will have a fair opportunity to talk. Otherwise, members will interrupt each other to get the floor in order to give their views.

Avoid Procedural Skirmishes

Sometimes a member, perhaps in an effort to impede the group or perhaps in an honest attempt to set the meeting straight, will begin to use parliamentary procedure negatively. That member may call for a point of order or for personal privilege or challenge a procedural decision of the group to limit discussion. The use of legalisms to torpedo a meeting's progress is an old tactic that you should try to recognize quickly. It is wise not to get involved with such procedural maneuvers when they are aimed at hindering the meeting and provoking argumentation. They will deter you from dealing with the substantive issue before the group, which is the reason for meeting in the first place.

Participate Discreetly

As a faculty member, you have the right to participate and you have the obligation to your colleagues to let them know how you stand on the issues which face the group. However, you must use discretion so that you don't monopolize the discussion on the motion nor use unfair advantage of your position as chairperson to dominate the discussion. Since you are chairperson, your words are powerful and consequently you do not need to speak often or long. Speak out but speak discreetly. You need not be merely a procedural machine who conducts the meeting but says nothing substantive. You need not act like the vice-president of the United States, who serves as president of the Senate but does not have a vote except when there is a tie vote of the senators themselves.

Lobby Judiciously

This item, though listed last, actually connects with the first item, "Be prepared." You cannot lobby during the meeting but you can do so before the meeting. If you know that certain agenda items will evoke motions, it is not only permissible but judicious and prudent to speak with faculty members ahead of time. Before the meeting, you can alert them to a forthcoming motion and seek their support. This is permissible since you will be speaking discreetly at the meeting, as mentioned earlier. It is prudent to do so as you lead your faculty in order to avoid unnecessary acrimony and misunderstanding at the meeting.

A Chart of Motions

To help yourself with main motions, amendments, and other types of motions, see Figure 1-2. It summarizes, in easy-reference form, the information you will need as you deal with most of the motions faced in a faculty meeting.

TO VOTE OR NOT TO VOTE

It is almost natural in our democracy to think of voting when thinking about meetings. We have grown up cherishing our democratic heritage and the right to vote on issues that directly affect us. However, since our small town meetings have expanded, now we vote for representatives to our state and national governments who vote on our behalf as they represent our interests. In our large civic organizations and business corporations, we vote on overall policy issues. In many ways, we have come to assume that voting is the *only* possible or naturally best way to arrive at a decision. Such an assumption is false; it is harmful, too, in that it limits our thinking about decision making. Moreover, it may prevent us from employing other ways to decide that may be better suited to a particular group at a particular point in time.

To Vote

There are, indeed, good reasons for using voting as the process for deciding. As already noted, we have a deep-rooted tradition in our democracy that supports and favors voting. People have grown up with voting and are accustomed to use it as the way to decide between two candidates for office or between two sides (yes/no) of a proposal for action. Voting is a comfortable process and doesn't require learning new decision-making skills.

Voting in a meeting to decide between two sides of an issue is analogous to our deciding in court between two litigants. Just as the jury must decide "guilty or not guilty" in a murder case and appellate judges must "affirm or reverse" the trial court's decision, the members voting on a policy motion must choose between favoring or opposing. In each case, the choice is between two opposites. In essence, the choice offered to people who decide is between yes or no. In a murder trial the question is, "Is the defendant guilty of the charge brought against him?" For a motion, the proposal is put in the form of a question, too: "Do you support this proposed motion?" (It is for this reason that a member who wants to stop discussion calls "the previous question" and that the chairperson calls for those in favor to say "Aye" or "Yes" and those opposed to say "No." The Constitution of the United States uses the words "Yes" and "Nay.") In each case, the answer is a clear cut yes or no. People are willing and prepared to vote this way because they have become accustomed to doing so when deciding in a group, and the parallel with our court system, which they support, is apparent to them implicitly.

Another advantage to the voting process, especially voting yes or no on a motion, is the simplicity for the discussion that precedes the actual voice or hand vote. The member needs only to decide between two alternatives, choosing between taking action or not. There is no need to decide between three or four simultaneous proposals, either A or B or C or none. One and only one proposal faces the member at any moment. If a motion is defeated, someone can move another motion calling for a different action. Neverthe-

Type	Purpose	May interrupt speaker without first being recognized by chairperson?	Need to be seconded?	Discussable?	Amendable?	Vote Required?
Main motion	Introduces proposed action	No	Yes	Yes	Yes	Majority[a]
Amend a motion	Modifies, revises main motion	No	Yes	Yes[b]	Yes	Majority
Adjourn	Ends meeting	No	Yes	No	No	Majority
Refer to committee	Asks for further study and recommendation	No	Yes	Yes	Yes	Majority
Limit or extend	Sets limits on discussion	No	Yes	No	Yes	Two-thirds
Previous question	Ends discussion on motion	No	Yes	No	No	Two-thirds
Lay on the table	Sets aside; postpones	No	Yes	No	No	Majority
Postpone to a definite time	Delays action and considers in future	No	Yes	Yes	Yes	Majority
Point of order	Enforces procedural rules	Yes	No	No[c]	No	None; chair decides
Request information (point of information)	Solicits or offers information	Yes	No	No	No	None necessary
Take from the table	Brings up for further consideration	No	Yes	No	No	Majority
Division of the house	Gets a counted vote	Yes	No	No	No	None; a demand of a single member requires a count to take place

[a] except when bylaws require more than a majority vote
[b] if the motion to be amended is discussable
[c] unless chairperson submits the question to the house

FIGURE 1-2. A chart of motions.

less, only one motion is before the group at a time, and the member votes to support it (yes) or oppose it (no) only. Neat and clean.

Not to Vote

Voting as a decision-making process has some distinct disadvantages. First, voting creates and maintains a win/lose environment. When voting we talk of victory and defeat, winning and losing. The terminology comes from war, where the powerful person or army emerges with a victory or win. (Competitive sports employ the same terminology as they draw upon the war metaphor, too.) This win/lose frame of mind is not a healthy one for a group that also seeks and needs *internal* cooperation and cohesion. It simply is not good for group spirit to have the win/lose environment pervading the internal decisions facing the members.

Voting on a main motion requires only a majority of members to support a proposal in order to commit the entire group to action. Yet the "winning" group may be only two (for example, fifty-one to forty-nine) or even one (for example, five to four) person greater than the "losing" group. In this way, on an important issue virtually one-half of the group supports the action but commits the entire group to that action. Often, the "losing" group is angry, dissatisfied, and without a close personal stake—ownership—in that particular issue. One-half of the group may not act wholeheartedly or may not even act at all if they feel "defeated in battle."

Furthermore, voting on one issue at a time in terms of supporting or favoring the motion allows members to gloss over the subtle gray areas between the two opposite sides. Putting the question in terms of two extremes, yes or no, doesn't encourage people to meet together on common ground. The simple world of yes/no in voting often doesn't reflect the complex world of action, where more than one possibility faces the decision-maker at a given moment of time. When voting for candidates for public office, we often have more than two choices. However, for motions at a meeting (and even when voting on bond issues in a public voting booth) we have but two choices, yes and no, though we might wish some gray options to modify the main motion.

Alternatives to Deciding by Majority Vote

There is little doubt that voting is desirable in large groups. "How else?" you might well ask. There are two aspects of deciding by majority vote that can be altered. First, since there is no divine commandment that we must decide by 51 percent or more of a given group, we could easily decide to require a two-thirds majority or even a three-fourths majority. The two-thirds- and three-fourths-majority votes are used in our public lives. For example, the U.S. Constitution requires a two-thirds vote of the House of Representatives to propose an Amendment. It also requires three-fourths of the state legislatures to ratify a proposed Amendment. Furthermore, to override a President's veto of a bill, a two-thirds vote of both houses of Congress is required. The increase from a simple majority to a two-thirds or three-fourths majority assures that in a group of nine or seventeen, for example, a five to four or nine to eight split is impossible. Such an increase indicates a strong support for a motion and thereby reduces some of the disadvantage of a simple majority vote.

Second, there are alternatives to the process of voting itself, whether the required majority be 51, or 67, or 75 percent. Such alternatives as delegation and consensus are often raised when we talk about small groups. That is, the question "To vote or not to vote?" arises most often when we begin to consider the size of the group, especially when we have a small group. Is a faculty of twenty so large that voting is the only real option? A faculty of fifteen? A faculty of ten? A faculty of seven? Obviously, somewhere along the slippery slope indicating the size of the faculty there is a shift from being *large* and requiring voting to being *small* and able to employ workable alternatives to voting such as delegation and consensus. Alternatives to voting are available to every faculty, but too many people believe that they work only in "small" rather than "large" groups. Nevertheless, even large faculties employ some forms of delegation and consensus.

Delegation as an Alternative to Voting

We use delegation in our daily lives when we say to a friend or spouse, "Okay, we'll go out to dinner tonight but you choose the restaurant." We also use delegation in our public government when the President delegates power to decide important issues to the Secretary of State, or the Attorney General, or the Environmental Protection Agency, for example. These new decision-makers are not selected by voting and have some executive power to decide as delegated to them by the President. That is, in delegation we request or agree that someone will decide for us.

Delegation works especially well when we can select the best person to decide for us and when there is rotation in the delegation of decision making. If Joe is an experienced hiker, we will most likely delegate him to decide for our hiking group which trail to take when we visit the Blue Ridge Mountains. If we go out to dinner regularly, we may well rotate who decides: "Last time you decided, so this time Mary decides which restaurant we should go to, and next time it's Fran's turn." We may wish to influence the delegated person's decision but the ultimate decision is made by the person delegated by the group.

Delegation can work well in a faculty where everyone has or will have an opportunity to decide for the group. It does not work well when only one or two people decide for the group all the time. Hence, it works well where there is a small group, where there is close contact among group members in order to offer advisory opinions, where the bond of trust is strong among members, and where there is rotation of delegated decision making. Rather than have the entire faculty—whatever its size—discuss where the ninth-grade students should go on this yearly class visit, the faculty can delegate either Chris Jones or Pat Smith or both to decide since they are trusted, ninth-grade teachers. It may foster faculty spirit more to delegate decision-making power to Jones and/or Smith than to risk the disadvantages associated with voting.

Delegation, therefore, has the advantages of (1) allowing those with special competence to use that competence for the betterment of the group, (2) developing the sense of contribution of faculty members to the group as a whole, (3) permitting members to grow and shine as they work on a particular issue, and (4) avoiding the win/ lose environment surrounding a given issue that might yield an extreme position without gray areas considered. Delegation is a usable alternative to voting when the faculty consciously sets out to use it for improved meetings and general operations.

Consensus as an Alternative to Voting

Consensus is another alternative to voting although some people see it only as a special instance of voting, namely, voting where there is 100 percent agreement. Consensus is an alternative to voting because it doesn't focus on yes/no but on finding common points on which people can agree. Consensus occurs when an initial proposal is modified to such an extent that everyone can accept in some way. Everyone has "ownership" of the proposal, and the win/lose environment of majority voting is avoided. In short, *consensus means general agreement on an issue that everyone can support somewhat.* It focuses on agreement, not win/lose or giving in, which are negative perspectives for staff development.

We use consensus in our daily lives even though we may not realize it or label it as such. For example, when we are with friends deciding on what to do at a seaside picnic, someone might suggest a barbecue of hamburgers and hot dogs to be preceded by a short badminton tournament. Several people suggest modifications such as a quick boat ride before the barbecue or badminton to be replaced by volleyball so that more people can participate. The final decision on which everyone agrees might be: a volleyball game between the Reds and the Greens, the barbecue, boat riding, and then swimming and singing of old-time favorites.

Consensus involves an interchange that allows and encourages people to speak their preferences and to offer modifications so that everyone can support the final agreement. Because people realize that reaching consensus is different from voting where two subgroups emerge, the yes group and the no group, the nature of the exchanges between them is supportive. There is no victor and no vanquished; everyone "wins" with consensus and thus the win/lose environment disappears. The environment is not even win/win because that implies two sides; rather the perspective is simply one of everyone winning.

Two disadvantages of consensus deserve attention amid the present praise for it. One, consensus is difficult in a large group (whatever "large" means), especially where people are not experienced with using this process for deciding. By difficult, I mean that people do not know how to speak about proposals or how to respond to disagreements with their own point of view. Because consensus requires many close and informal interchanges among people, "large" untrained groups find it awkward to use consensus. But what constitutes a "large" group for consensus is not at all clear at this point. Two, consensus consumes more time in order to reach a decision. It may not consume more time in the long run, however, because once the decision is reached there is little need for time to "heal wounds" or to "make the decision stick" since everyone has a stake in the decision reached.

CHAPTER 1 ENDNOTES

1. RICHARD J. DUNSING, *You and I Have Simply Got to Stop Meeting This Way* (New York: AMACOM, 1977), 29.
2. KING BROADRICK, *Parliamentary Procedure: Tool of Leadership* (Bloomington, IN: The Phi Delta Kappa Educational Foundation, 1974), 11.

┌──────┐
│   │
│ 2   │
│   │
└──────┴──────────────────────────────┐
       │   │
       │ *COLORED BROKEN*   │
       │   │
       │ *SQUARES*   │
       │   │
       │ *Cooperation and Communication* │
       │   │
       └──────────────────────────────┘

Based on a set of single-color figures by Bavelas[1], the Colored Broken Squares activity, though silent in its execution, speaks out loudly about the need for cooperation and communication in developmental supervision. The participants, in groups of five, demonstrate through their own work how cooperation is necessary among people who face problems together. Indeed, though some people may overlook it, the very act of doing this structured activity together is a cooperative endeavor. From their experience with the squares, the participants will be able to talk concretely about the need for cooperation and the connection between nonverbal communication and cooperation.

After reading this chapter, you should be able to:

- Understand the purpose of, steps for, and points raised by the Colored Broken Squares activity.
- Prepare the materials necessary for this structured activity.
- Conduct the Colored Broken Squares activity confidently with your faculty following the step-by-step strategy.
- Describe at least eight points generally raised in the debriefing discussion.
- Know how to apply the points raised by this activity in three different ways.

OVERVIEW

The Colored Broken Squares activity offers you the opportunity to inquire into cooperation, the roles of verbal and nonverbal communication, the assumptions which teachers hold, and the sensitivity that a leader needs in order to help his group. It is an excellent springboard for working in staff development. In this activity participants form small groups of five people and try to put together pieces of a puzzle to form a square in front of each participant. Participants proceed according to specific rules which are enforced by the leader and a specially appointed observer/enforcer. The debriefing session builds on experiences and feelings of the participants and the comments of the observers to examine the points raised by this activity.

MATERIALS NEEDED

For each small group of five people who will be involved in this activity, cut pieces from 4″ × 4″ sheets of colored oaktag or posterboard using the patterns shown in Figures 2-1, 2-2, and 2-3. You will have fifteen pieces in all, *each the same color on both sides*: three red, three blue, four green, three yellow, and two white. Place all the pieces of one color in the same envelope, five separate envelopes for each group of five people. Mark each envelope with the color and number of pieces to be found inside it.

NOTE: Figures 2-1, 2-2, and 2-3 are reprinted with permission of *Journal of the Acoustical Society of America.*

NUMBER OF PARTICIPANTS

You can do this activity with as few as five people. It is better to do it with at least fifteen so you can have three working groups of five each. You can do it with one or two groups but three to five groups are better. It is advisable to have at least one observer/enforcer in addition to the leader.

You should involve every person present. In order to involve extra people you can:

1. Assign them the role of observer/enforcer (a) to take mental and written notes of what they observe while a group tries to solve the puzzle and (b) to help you enforce the rules that you will announce to everyone. You can have several observer/enforcers if you wish. You should have at least one to serve as a source of external data.

2. Create Siamese twins. That is, ask two people to become one participant by sitting side-by-side, hooking arms that touch, and each working with one hand only; they will have two heads that do not talk to each other but only one set of arms.

3. Create jacks-in-the-box. That is, two people who work alternately as one participant. One stands behind the other. At a cue from you—after a few minutes— the jacks switch positions. The jack who was sitting pops up to take the place of the jack who was standing and vice versa. The former standing jack now works with the other participants in the group to solve the puzzle. The two jacks may not talk to each other. The two jacks should switch positions several times.

4. Create a musical chair participant. That is, the musical chair person starts out circulating and observing. After a few minutes upon a signal from you, the musical chair may tap any participant in any group and switch positions with that person. The new musical chair circulates, observes, and switches with someone else after a few minutes.

With these roles and others of your own creation, you can and should involve every person who is present. While you use at least five people to form a group to solve the puzzle, you can have one to four extra people for each group of five solvers and thus accommodate many people with just five sets of puzzle pieces.

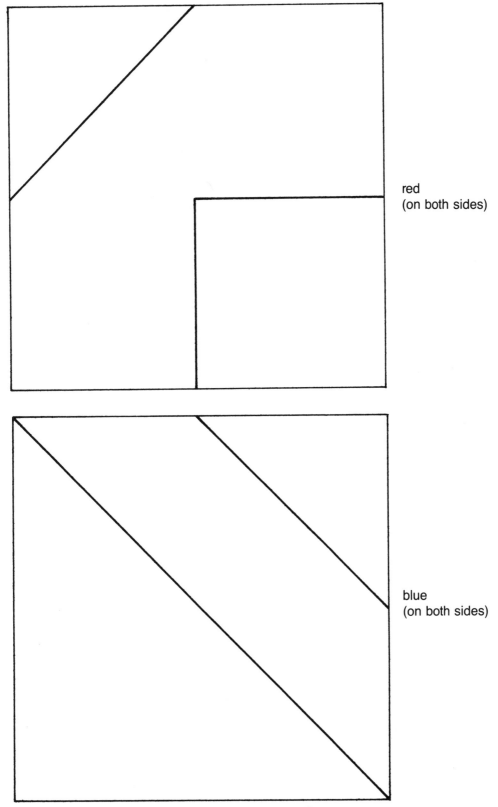

red
(on both sides)

blue
(on both sides)

FIGURE 2-1. Cutting patterns for Colored Broken Squares.

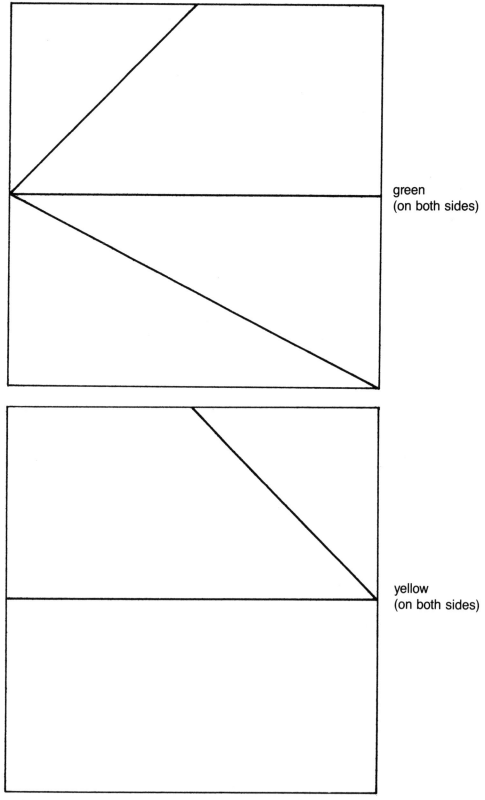

green
(on both sides)

yellow
(on both sides)

FIGURE 2-2. Cutting patterns for Colored Broken Squares.

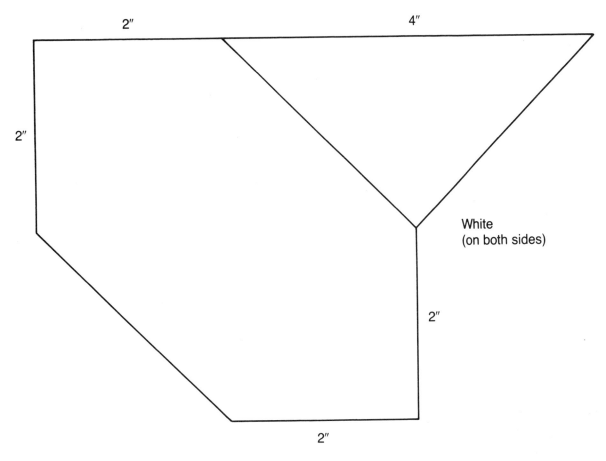

FIGURE 2-3. Cutting pattern for Colored Broken Squares.

PROCEDURE

Step 1. Distribute a set of five prepared envelopes to one person in each group of five participants. Ask that person not to open the envelopes; and ask that person to give out the envelopes only when you signal to do so shortly.

Step 2. Request the observers and others (musical chairs, for example) to position themselves near the various groups.

Step 3. *Read* the following instructions so that they will be precise and repeatable in the exact same way: "I have distributed among you envelopes containing pieces of a puzzle. Each group has its own complete set of five envelopes. These pieces will form five complete squares of equal dimensions with one of them to be placed in front of each member of your group. That is, each square will be the same size as each of the other four. Your task is to assemble a square in front of you. Each person is to assemble one square in front of him or her. You must observe these rules:

1. You may not ask for a piece from someone else in your group. This includes asking in any way, verbally or nonverbally. You may not signal, gesture, motion, take a piece, or in any other way try to get a piece from someone else in your group.
2. You may get a piece from someone else only if that person gives it to you.

3. If you give a piece to another person, you may not put it in place for him or her. You may only give someone else a piece and then that person must position that piece him- or herself.

4. You may give any of your pieces to any other group member. You may give away at any time all of your pieces, if you so wish. If you give away all of your pieces, you must do so one piece at a time; you may not give away your pieces assembled.

5. You may not talk at any time during this activity. The observer(s) will help me to enforce these rules as we note the actions of the participants in each group trying to make the five squares."

Step 4.   Ask one person in each group to distribute the five envelopes any way he or she wants, one to each participant.

Step 5.   Ask each group to open the envelopes and begin.

Step 6.   *Allow* time for each group to work on solving the puzzle. If you have a pair of jacks-in-the-box or a musical chair, *signal* them to switch positions after every three to four minutes. *Circulate* in order to observe the groups and to enforce the rules.

Step 7.   If the groups have not solved the puzzle after ten to fifteen minutes, you can ask them to "freeze." Then ask them to walk silently around the room for one minute to see what the other *unsuccessful* groups have done. Then they should return to their seats to continue as before. This is an optional step; it has the advantage of releasing some tension among unsuccessful groups and of giving the participants a break.

Step 8.   As the groups succeed, you can announce that you are giving some extra time to the "slow" group. If you do use this optional tactic, quietly clue in your observer(s) and successful groups beforehand as to your intention so they can observe the reaction of the "slow" group to your label of them. Their observations on the "slow" group's reaction to the label will be a good point for the debriefing discussion to follow. Furthermore, you can notify the last group still trying to solve the puzzle that it can talk. This will likely lead to a speedy solution. You can raise this point in the discussion later, too.

Step 9.   After all the groups have solved the puzzle (see Figure 2-4 for the solution) or after you have halted the activity (some or even all may still be unsuccessful), you should begin a debriefing discussion. As you debrief, try to keep your role as discussion facilitator and paraphraser. Try not to "preach" to the group. Patience will pay off.

Read through the section entitled "Points Raised by Activity" to alert yourself to the points that generally come out during this discussion. (The points are presented later because it is helpful and necessary for you to first have an idea of how people perform this activity in order to appreciate those points.) Do not try to force more points than the group is willing to initiate because the forced points probably will not be meaningful anyway. Keep the extra points in mind, note them, and use some other activities in this book to help bring them to your faculty.

Note that there are many sample questions below. You will no doubt not need to ask every question since many of the points will come to the floor without your solicitation. Ask only those questions you want to ask and need to ask in order to keep the discussion going.

FIGURE 2-4. Solution to Colored Broken Squares.

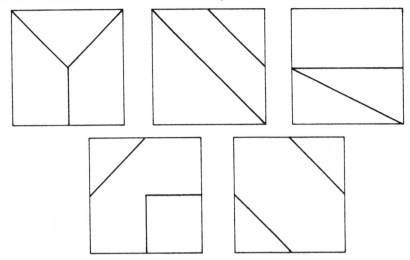

Follow the debriefing strategy presented here so you can reap the benefits of Colored Broken Squares:

1. Shift into the debriefing session by simply and only saying something like, "Now, let's talk about what happened so far."

2. Begin the discussion by encouraging the participants to *describe what happened*. Let them all "ventilate." Without sufficient hard-fact ventilation, there will not be an adequate basis for making discoveries and drawing conclusions later on. This opening phase of the debriefing will loosen up the participants and get them talking, as it is very easy to talk on this concrete, nonthreatening level. *Be sure to call on the observers to give a report*. Ask such questions as: What did you do when you first opened your envelope? How long did it take before you began to break up your squares and give away pieces? How did you feel when someone else had a piece you needed but didn't pass it to you? What was your reaction when someone made a square and then sat back without realizing that his square held others back from a solution? How did you feel when you had to break up your solution and give away pieces in order to help others find a solution? How did you feel about someone who misunderstood the directions and thus held everyone back from completing the five squares? How closely did you follow the rules? Were participants willing to cooperate by giving away pieces? What was your reaction to being labeled the "slow" group? Was it possible *not* to communicate to others about your need? Did you make any initial assumptions? If so, when did you give them up? Were participants cooperative or competitive?

3. *Analyze the meaning (purpose, points, or messages) of this activity*. Discuss what all of the action adds up to, what the point of the activity is. Ask such questions as: What does this all mean to you? What key ideas does this activity present to us? What did you learn about yourself and others from participating in this activity? What do the results teach us?

4. *Examine the implications of this activity for teaching and supervision*. Ask such questions as: Are there parallels between this activity and teaching? Are there any parallels between this activity and supervision? What applications do you see for us based on all of these points? In what ways can we change our classroom activities as a result of what we have learned from participating in this structured activity? In what ways can we modify our supervision procedures as a result of what we have learned from participating in this structured activity?

5. *Summarize, generalize, and conclude.* Tie the many points together—the messages, the parallels, and the implications. Do not assume that the participants will generalize and draw conclusions on their own without guidance. Ask such questions as: From all we have said and done, what conclusions do you draw from this activity? What can you say to summarize what we have said today?

   If you wish, you can do the summarizing in a different way. You can request the group to list some key ideas that have come forth during the discussion and to offer some generalizations based on these key ideas. This approach is effective since the generalizations grow immediately and directly from what the group says. You can initiate this approach by asking each person to complete whichever of the following sentence stems you feel is more appropriate:

Based on this activity, I realize about teaching that_____

_____.

Based on this activity, I realize about supervision that_____

_____.

Be sure to ask the group to read their completed sentences.

Step 10.   To embellish on the points raised during your debriefing discussion, you can try this activity again. If you do, then vary slightly some of the elements. For example, group the participants differently; ask observers to become solvers and vice versa; give special roles to other people; distribute the fifteen pieces randomly; cut the pieces from cardboard of a single color. You can move to this "replay" after Step 9(3) or 9(4) of the debriefing. After the replay, continue on with your debriefing session. In the debriefing, discuss how the second group utilized ideas learned in the first attempt and the early part of the discussion.

Step 11.   Move forward. Before leaving Colored Broken Squares behind, structure the situation so that you launch yourself and the group into something new built on it. In this way, you bridge current activity with future activity while interest is high. For example, you might schedule your next meeting as a time to plan and implement ideas. Suggest that you will provide a summary just to get the meeting off to a good start. See the "Applications" section for further ideas.

POINTS RAISED BY ACTIVITY

It may be difficult for you as you read through this description of Colored Broken Squares to realize just what people will say during the solving phase and the debriefing phase. To help you, below are a dozen essential points that generally come up during this activity. You may find some others as well. By familiarizing yourself with these points you will know what to expect and also be able to see how this activity can help you in your supervision duties. There is some overlap among the points that follow, but that is to be expected since they all arise from this one activity. Yet each is worthy of mention.

   1.   *We must take care in making assumptions especially regarding actions that affect other group members.* This point arises because some participants assume (incorrectly) that the color of a piece matters. Indeed, color is insignificant; only shape counts. By assuming that color counts, people inhibit their actions. The false assumption affects their actions as they seek to find a solution.

Similarly, teachers and supervisors make assumptions in regard to supervision that are false and inhibit their actions. All too often, people assume that a particular teacher is not interested in further development as a professional; or, they assume that a particular supervisor cannot learn new skills of observing and conferring. By acting on such assumptions, they hinder supervision and then mistake cause and effect. It is necessary, therefore, to ask ourselves frequently: What is the basis for our actions? Where are our assumptions leading us? Are there different ways to think about this? If we assume B instead of A, what will be the implications? In what ways can we alter what is happening by starting with a different—perhaps more valid—set of assumptions and beliefs?

2. *Only when we challenge our assumptions and give up false, irrelevant, insignificant, or restricting ideas can we proceed to accomplish our goal.* This point is similar to the first one but goes beyond it. Some people assume initially in Colored Broken Squares that each of the five squares to be formed must be made up of one color only. This assumption holds them back. Only if the solvers give up this assumption, break up their squares, and begin to share pieces with each other can the group succeed with its task. The goal of five squares of equal dimensions cannot be accomplished if solvers— or even one crucial person—continues to believe that color is important. Color in this activity is a red herring.

When we believe that a new approach to observing or a new set of skills for conferring has potential to bring about change, we can start on the road to professional development. When we give up the idea that a particular teacher is beyond help, we can seek ways that suit that teacher. It may be difficult to help veteran teachers to learn new ways of teaching, but when change occurs, the reward repays the effort. Until we change our approach, we impede ourselves. We need to take the initial step by giving up self-imposed assumptions. The belief that change is impossible is as much a restriction as the belief that color counts in this structured activity.

3. *To accomplish a group goal each individual must understand the total situation and the group goals.* If a participant in a group only cares about his own small section, he may impede the progress of the entire group. Only when a person sees the big picture does he function well with others. Each member of a group must understand the group's goal and keep it in mind in order for the group to succeed.

4. *Being willing to cooperate and share is essential when you are a member of a group or else the group cannot succeed.* If a group member will not share, very often the group cannot or will not succeed. In this activity, if the participants with green or yellow or white pieces do not share their pieces, the group cannot find a solution. Sharing is necessary.

5. *Teachers and supervisors should not wait for people to ask for help; they must be sensitive to the need for help and offer it even without an explicit request for it.* A person who is in charge of a group cannot sit back and wait for formal requests—cannot sit on ceremony. When our lives are linked directly, as in teaching and supervising, we need to help each other. But we must not wait for others to recognize their need and make formal requests for help. In this activity, a person who has a need for a piece cannot ask for it and the person who holds back offering help hurts the group.

A teacher or supervisor must recognize the needs and talents of the group. Then they must act to help the members of the group to make their maximum contribution to the group and even themselves. Each person ideally must anticipate the requests that others will make and offer services voluntarily. This does not mean that we must tell people what their needs are or that they have problems. Rather, it means offering help, and this may mean to help them recognize the need or problem so that they are ready to accept help.

6. *Our manner communicates messages to others.* Even when we do not talk verbally with our voices, we "talk" with our bodies and our actions. We always are communicating. In this activity the rule calls for the participants not to ask for a piece verbally or nonverbally by signal or gestures. In a sense, it is impossible to obey this rule since we always communicate our needs. Though you may not say "I need that piece" or gesture with your hands to request a piece, your body may communicate your need even though you are not conscious of it. People never stop communicating; on some level everyone is always communicating.

7. *Successful group collaboration can produce a feeling of unity which can stimulate a feeling of power. This feeling of power in turn can evoke good feelings within individual group members.* When a group succeeds there is a synergistic effect. The combined efforts of the members yields a new effect which, like two drugs taken together, is greater than the separate parts. The feeling of group success and power that comes from the individual members returns to the individuals to give them a sense of power and confidence they did not have previously.

8. *It is frustrating not to be able to talk.* People talk naturally, and when they must not talk when working together, they become frustrated. Talking is a natural human activity.

9. *It is frustrating not to be able to tell other people how to solve their problems.* We are quite accustomed to helping others by telling them what to do. When we cannot, we feel frustrated. In this activity, a person cannot give an assembled square to someone else, nor can he tell someone where and how to use a piece given away. A person must rely on the receiver to use a piece correctly. If a person sees a piece being used improperly or given away unnecessarily, frustration, and perhaps even annoyance or anger, sets in.

10. *A group working on a task can be influenced by an observer.* Since people working on a task are often tense and intent, the presence of an observer can distract them or make them self-conscious. The effect may be to reduce the group's ability to concentrate and to succeed.

11. *A group can be affected by the progress or achievement of another group.* When a group sees how others groups behave (see Step 7 for letting people see what others are doing), it can renew its efforts to succeed. It can build on what it learns from others. In addition, a group can feel failure or embarrassment when it is the last group to succeed or the only one not to succeed. This is especially so if the group is publicly labeled as slow. (See Step 8 for this possibility.) Even though no competition is built into this activity explicitly, some groups feel competitive and act accordingly as they note who has succeeded and who has not.

12. *Like the pieces of the squares, students and teachers come in various shapes, sizes, and colors, each different, and each has his or her own needed role to play in the situation.* Everyone counts; everyone has worth; it is our job to help people find their places so that they can contribute their talents to the whole.

SUGGESTIONS AND COMMENTS

1. Before doing this activity with your faculty, try it out with a few select friends just to get the hang of it. Try it as a social, parlor activity at your home. All you need is a minimum of five people to gain experience. Besides getting the feel of the activity, you will have a fun evening with your friends. This tryout session is especially suggested if you have little previous experience with such small group interaction.

2. Follow the given strategy at least the first few times. It will give you support. It is one that has proven successful many times already. Once you are comfortable with structured activity, feel free to modify anything and everything to fit your needs.

3. You can conduct the entire activity in one hour if you move rapidly. If you have more time, you can go slowly and use up to two hours easily. If you must go fast, speed up in Step 5 through Step 8. But leave at least forty minutes for Step 9 and Step 11. These steps are most important since they bring home the message.

4. If you are a superintendent, for example, and do not feel comfortable in leading this activity with your faculty, by all means ask someone else to lead it. Perhaps a particular principal, a guidance counselor, or a central-office curriculum coordinator would be an excellent person to be the leader. You can be a participant or observer, as you see fit.

APPLICATIONS

Colored Broken Squares is not an end in itself. As stated earlier, it is an excellent springboard for working with your teachers in staff development. The activity will provide motivation and key ideas regarding the concepts of cooperation, assumptions, and communication. It is then necessary for you to build on this activity. You can direct the application activities toward the classroom if you are working with teachers; or, you can direct the application activities toward supervision if you are working with fellow supervisors. In either case, you can build easily since the points apply to both teaching and supervision. Several suggestions follow:

SPECIAL MEMO

One simple way to follow up on the Colored Broken Squares session is to send a memo to your entire staff highlighting the points raised. Figure 2-5 is an easy one to use as a quick and effective method for informing your faculty about your views on the session. An example of a completed form is shown in Figure 2-6. Here the supervisor picks up on two key quotes regarding communication in the top part and the need for cooperation and group success in the middle part. He uses the bottom part to raise questions, especially the one which asks if the faculty wants to become and act like a group rather than a collection of individuals each, perhaps, going along with different goals.

TO: _____

FROM: _____

RE: Follow-up from Colored Broken Squares

    Led by _____ on _____, 19___

1. Quotable quotes from the session:

    A.

    B.

    C.

2. Key points raised:

    A.

    B.

    C.

3. Decisions to follow through for implementation:

FIGURE 2-5. Follow-up memo for Colored Broken Squares (blank).

TO: _____ Faculty _____

FROM: _____ Chuck Stegner _____

RE: Follow-up from Colored Broken Squares

Led by _____ Chuck _____ on _____ Sept. 1 , 19 XX

1. Quotable quotes from the session:

   A. Adrienne: People naturally need to talk.

   B. Maryann: Even if they can't talk out loud, they'll talk to each other silently, like with their eyes.

   C. Diane: Observers make me nervous.

2. Key points raised:

   A. Successful group collaboration can produce a feeling of unity which can stimulate a feeling of power.

   B. A willingness on each member's part to share is necessary to the accomplishment of a group goal.

   C. In order to successfully complete a group task, each person needs to understand what the group goal is.

3. Decisions to follow through for implementation:

   Let's ask ourselves: Do we understand what our goal implies for each of us? What is the responsibility each of us has to the others? Are we willing to become a group? Each one of us has to give to the students and to the faculty or we won't succeed. Others are asking. Are we answering?

FIGURE 2-6. Follow-up memo for Colored Broken Squares (filled in).

The purpose of the memo is twofold. First, it alerts the faculty to your view of the session by offering in concrete, written form what was talked about in the debriefing discussion. Second, it serves as a springboard for faculty thinking. Each person will think of these points individually and then together as a combined staff. The follow-up memo serves as a springboard because you have provided the faculty with the necessary material before you begin a new session in which they will be involved with the implementation of ideas.

SPECIAL STAFF MEETING

Suppose you schedule a special session with your teaching faculty to work on the application of the ideas from Colored Broken Squares to supervision. You might begin with the question, "What common goals do we share regarding supervision?" Once you all have identified what you share in common, you can ask for *specific* ways that the teachers can cooperate—each contributing his special skills and knowledge—to help the others in accomplishing this goal. Ask for actions that they can take which will lead to change and show that change is occurring.

The key here is to elicit specific actions that the faculty can take in order to respond to individual needs. You might get such answers as: sharing effective teaching tactics; peer observations; cooperative or consultative unit planning; mutual diagnosis of student learning strengths and weaknesses when teachers have the same student in class; and some guest teaching for teachers now teaching alone. No matter what it is, it is important for you to see this as a first step toward the faculty acting as a group with shared goals and responsibilities.

In order to eliminate or reduce resistance to the changes that such a procedure may bring into the lives of your teachers, it is important for you carefully to guide the faculty in the next phase, too. The teachers should do two things in order to increase the likelihood that change will occur. First, they should *themselves gather the data* necessary for demonstrating the need for change—if any further data are needed. They already have generated some data through their participation in the structured activity. That is, for example, if they want to know what various members have as their goals for supervision, they themselves should construct the questionnaire and conduct the survey.

Second, the group should *decide on its own how to implement any decisions* made regarding changes needed by the staff. You should not gather data for them. Nor should you decide how and when to implement steps designed to effect change. The staff will be more accepting of change if it gathers its own data and then decides how to implement its own decisions based on those data.

INDIVIDUAL CONFERENCES

You may wish to meet with your staff individually as you seek to build on the Colored Broken Squares activity. Here, too, it is helpful to begin with a brief review of the points raised during the activity, especially those raised by the person with whom you are conferring. By focusing on what that person did and said and by relating the ideas to that person's particular strengths you can together think of areas for change.

Together you can list what that teacher, for example, can contribute to the group regarding peer observation and demonstrating effective teaching tactics. You can list also what the teacher can ask of the other members of the group. What teaching techniques will the teacher demonstrate as a master teacher? What does the teacher wish to observe as a way of learning additional effective teaching tactics? Who will the teacher be willing to observe and confer with? Whom would the teacher welcome as an observer? What would the teacher want a fellow teacher to observe? Is the teacher willing to video record a teaching session for others and you to learn from? Is the teacher willing to conduct an in-service program that can involve the others in a learning situation?

The emphasis should be on cooperation, on giving, and on taking. It should be on creating a sense of sharing so that the teacher can benefit by receiving as well as giving. The emphasis should not be on what the teacher needs to give up—that is, assumptions and actions which hinder change. Rather, the teacher, through the conference with you, should feel that he or she is an active agent who can change by taking positive action. The teacher should feel active by contributing, by giving help, and by receiving help. Such action leads to greater cooperation for mutual benefit.

CONCLUDING WORDS

Colored Broken Squares is a powerful activity. While it engages your faculty in a playful manner, it raises significant issues which directly apply to supervision. There are at least a dozen important points which you can discuss with your staff, each with a potential for leading you to new areas for change. It is necessary for you to seize the opportunity to talk with your staff about these points and to plan with them what actions you can all do together. The staff, by participating in the activity from solving through debriefing, will take significant steps toward becoming a group that can cooperate for the increased benefit of all concerned, including you.

CHAPTER 2 ENDNOTE

1. ALEX BAVELAS, "Communication Patterns in Task-Oriented Groups," *Journal of the Acoustical Society of America,* Vol. 22 (1950): 725–730.

3

THE PENNY

Observation, Inference,

and Evaluation

This activity concerns three major processes and skills that are present in your daily activities as a supervisor. Indeed, the various state and local laws require supervisors to observe their faculty members in order to establish the foundation of the conferences to be held and the reports to be written. Therefore, it is most important that you understand what observing is and what are some questions raised when looking below the surface at some proposed observations. From their experience with The Penny, the participants will gain an understanding of as well as a sensitivity to observing as the cornerstone of your relationship with the faculty.

After reading this chapter, you should be able to:

- Understand the purpose of, steps for, and points raised by The Penny.
- Gather the materials necessary for this structured activity.
- Conduct The Penny confidently with your faculty by following the step-by-step strategy presented.
- Describe at least three points generally raised in the discussion held with the participants.
- Know how to apply the points raised by this structured activity in three different ways.

OVERVIEW

The Penny is deceptively simple. You use as the focus of the participants' attention a common, everyday object which we all take for granted and hardly ever examine. Based on what the participants report that they have observed you proceed to explore with the group what constitutes an observation and what does not, what constitutes an inference, and what constitutes an evaluation. The purpose is to highlight the differences between the processes of observing, inferring, and evaluating, which are three processes fundamental to the supervising of teachers. By first exploring the three processes in regard to a penny, the participants are prepared to discuss the complexities of observing, inferring, and evaluating faculty members.

MATERIALS NEEDED

For each participant you will need a new shiny penny. All of the pennies should be of the same date and same mint mark (that is, either no mint mark or the same mint mark under the year of the coin). You will also need three to five variant pennies which vary from the ones you will use in general: (1) a penny that is not new and is scratched or otherwise hard to observe in detail; (2) a penny dated before 1959 so it will have a different reverse side (tails); (3) a penny with a different mint mark (for example, if you use a 1984 penny with no letter under the date to indicate the place of minting, then obtain a penny which has a "D" for Denver or "S" for San Francisco under the year); (4) a penny with a different date but with the same mint mark; (5) a Canadian penny; and (6) an Indian Head penny, the penny which preceded the Lincoln penny. You should also have a magnifying glass, a ruler or micrometer, a delicate scale that is capable of weighing a penny, and a piece of paper and a pencil for each person. (Keep the magnifying glass, ruler, micrometer, and scale out of sight.)

NUMBER OF PARTICIPANTS

You can do this activity with as few as four people. It is better to do it with ten or more participants because then you will have a richer source of observations to work with and an opportunity to have small groups of participants compare their observations before the discussion with the whole group. In short, you can do this activity with just about any number of participants.

PROCEDURE

Step 1.   Distribute a penny to each person. *Do not* use the words "penny" or "coin" at this point since neither word appears officially on the penny. Simply distribute a penny to each person and refer to it as an object or item. That is, use a generic term to refer to the penny. (See "Suggestions and Comments" for possible use of the variant pennies in this step.)

Step 2.   Request participants to record their "observations" of the "object" on a piece of paper. Ask them to *list as many observations* as they can on their paper and not to be concerned with any particular order. Participants should do this individually. Make sure here that you explicitly use the words "observe" and "observations." ("Please observe the object I've given to you. List as many observations as you can on your piece of paper. We'll use these observations shortly.")

Step 3. Ask participants to form pairs or trios and to compare their lists of observations. If you want, you can ask each small group to prepare a combined list of observations as a result of the comparisons.

Step 4. List on a chalkboard, overhead projector, or large easel pad fifteen to twenty-five observations made by the participants. As the participants offer you an observation, record it. Do not comment on it. See Figure 3-1 for a sample list of observations one group of eighteen teachers recently offered in just a few minutes. The group stopped at twenty-five observations; they said that they had more to offer.

Step 5. Go through the list, preferably in the order given, asking the group if each item is an observation. That is, since you requested participants to record and offer observations, you now need to check with the group to see if all the items listed on the chalkboard are observations. *This is the crucial step in the strategy* because here various participants will agree and disagree as to whether an item is indeed an observation. For example, in Figure 3-1 there was no fuss as to whether an item was an observation until we reached Item 9. Here several people said that it was not an observation to say that the man is Abraham Lincoln. The same was said of Items 16 and 17. That is, some people said that we can observe that it is a building, but we cannot observe that it is the Lincoln Memorial (which it is rather than the U.S. Treasury Building). Once the group begins to discuss in such terms—this item is an observation but another item is not—you should then focus the discussion on the list of items as to what distinguishes an *observation* from a nonobservation. (To guide you in this discussion see Point 1 in "Points Raised by Activity.")

Step 6. Before leaving the concept of observation you should deal with a statement like Item 25 in Figure 3-1, "There is no letter as a mint mark." The question here for you to raise is, "Is it possible to observe what doesn't exist?" In other words, "Is Item 25 an observation or something else?" If Item 25 is not an observation (because you cannot observe what is not present), then what is it? Item 25 is actually a conclusion which may pass as an observation because in its form it closely resembles an observation statement. It is a conclusion in that the person who made it knew of the possibility of a letter as a mint mark and did not find one. Based on the prior knowledge and consideration of the observations made about the penny the person drew a conclusion. A statement like Item 25 is clearly based on prior knowledge, and for this reason could not be made by a person unfamiliar with pennies.

If you do not have such a statement in your list but would like to raise this issue anyhow, you can easily modify the list. You can add such a statement or you can modify one that already is on the list. For example, you could modify items as follows:

7. There is no "Justice" to go along with "Liberty" (as in "Liberty and Justice for All").
9. The famous top hat of Lincoln's is not shown.
14. "Penny," the common word for this "one cent" object, does not appear.

Step 7. Another point about observation needs to be addressed, and you can do so easily by using your magnifying glass, ruler, or scale. Suppose that you decide to use the magnifying glass and that you have before you the list in Figure 3-1. Point out that no one has observed that there is an image of Lincoln sitting on his chair in the center of the

1. Round (Circular)

2. Flat

3. Copper colored

4. Size—about 3/4″ radius

5. Size—about 1/16″ thick

6. One date—1983

7. The word "Liberty" appears

8. Hair of man parted on right side

9. Picture (image) of Abraham Lincoln

10. Lincoln wearing a tie

11. Lincoln shown with head and shoulders and a beard

12. Viewer sees right side of Lincoln's face

13. It's a beautiful coin

14. The words "one cent"

15. The words "one cent" written in capital letters

16. Picture of a building—the Federal Treasury Building

17. Picture of the Lincoln Memorial

18. It's not worth much now in today's inflation

19. USA is written out

20. The words "E Pluribus Unum"

21. 3 different size letters on back: largest is One Cent; smallest is E Pluribus Unum; middle is United States of America

22. The words "In God We Trust"

23. The coin is shiny

24. The coin is cold—cold to the nose

25. There is no letter as a mint mark

FIGURE 3-1. Sample observations from The Penny.

building on the reverse side (tails) of the coin. It is difficult to see with the naked eye and especially difficult on a worn coin. However, with a magnifying glass and a new coin the image is fairly easy to see. Or, you can point out that the initials of the coin's designer appear on the penny and that no one saw them. With a new coin and a magnifying glass you can see the letters VDB on the raised bevel of Lincoln's right shoulder. The initials stand for Victor D. Brenner, who designed the penny.

You may then ask if the following two statements made only with the aid of a magnifying glass can count as observations:

1.   There is an image of Lincoln sitting in his chair as part of the image of the Lincoln Memorial building.
2.   The letters VDB appear on the raised bevel of the right shoulder of Lincoln (the man whose image appears on the penny).

That is, if we need to use a tool of some sort to enhance our senses, does a statement made possible by that tool count as an observation? Or, must observations be made only with our five unaided senses? May a person use eyeglasses? A hearing aid? A ruler to measure length? A scale to measure weight?

Step 8.   Once you have identified the items which qualify as observations according to the agreement you reach with the group about the concept of observation, then begin a discussion on the other items. Here you should begin by examining the items that were almost accepted as observations or items that are true but do not qualify as observations. For example, in Figure 3-1, Item 18 is not an observation, yet it is true. You thus will begin to deal with items which are inferences. (To guide you in this discussion see Point 1 in "Points Raised by Activity.")

Step 9.   After you have dealt with inferences you should deal with any generalizations and evaluations that might appear on the list offered by the participants. In Figure 3-1 there is no item that is a generalization, but there is one which is an evaluation. Item 13, "It's a beautiful coin," is an evaluative statement rather than an observation. Here is an excellent opportunity to discuss what makes a statement an evaluative one and the need for stating explicitly the criteria that allow us to say that the penny is a beautiful coin.

You may not be fortunate enough to get an evaluative statement on your list, but you should be prepared to treat one if it appears. If you do not get a generalization or an evaluative statement, you can enter into a discussion of such items by hypothetically modifying statements already on the list and asking the participants to comment on the "new" items. For example, you could modify Items 1, 2, and 5 as follows to get some generalizations:

1.   Pennies are round.
2.   Pennies are flat.
5.   Each coin is about 1/16" thick.

You could modify Items 10, 17, and 22 as follows to get some evaluations:

10.   Lincoln is shown as a handsome man wearing a tie.
17.   There's a beautiful picture of the Lincoln Memorial.
22.   It's a good idea to have the words "In God We Trust" on the penny.

Step 10.   After you have discussed observations, inferences, generalizations, and evaluations, summarize the discussion so far. One excellent way to do so is to offer some definitions which derive from your discussion. (See Point 1 in "Points Raised by Activity.") Refer to your specific discussion as you offer your definitions.

Step 11.   Continue the discussion by asking the participants to comment on the implications of this activity of observing the penny for teaching and supervising. Ask such questions as: Are there parallels between this activity and teaching? Are there parallels between this activity and supervision? What applications do you see for us based on the distinctions made among observing, inferring, generalizing, and evaluating? In what ways can we modify our supervision procedures as a result of what we have learned from participating in this structured activity?

Step 12.   Summarize, generalize, and conclude. Tie the many points together— the definitions, the points raised, the parallels, and the implications. Do not assume that the participants will generalize and draw conclusions on their own without guidance. Ask such questions as: From all we have said and done, what conclusions do you draw from this Penny activity? What can you say to summarize what we have said and done today?

If you wish, you can do the summarizing in a different way. You can request the group to list some key ideas that have come forth during the discussion and to offer some generalizations based on these key ideas. This approach is effective since the generalizations grow immediately and directly from what the group says. You can initiate this approach by asking each person to complete whichever of the following sentence stems you feel is more appropriate:

Based on this activity, I realize about teaching that

_____

Based on this activity, I realize about supervision that

_____

Be sure to ask the group to read their completed sentences.

Step 13.   Move forward. Before leaving The Penny activity behind, structure the situation so that you launch yourself and the group into something new built on the day's activity. In this way you bridge current activity with future activity while interest is high. For example, you might schedule a meeting to review your current supervisory form to see if there are clear distinctions drawn in it regarding observations, inferences, and evaluations. Suggest that you will prepare a summary sheet of today's activity just to get the scheduled meeting off to a good start. (See "Applications" for further ideas.)

POINTS RAISED BY ACTIVITY

It may be somewhat difficult for you as you read through this description of The Penny to realize just what people will say during the discussion phase. To help you, below are five essential points that generally come up during this activity. By familiarizing yourself with these points you will know what to expect and also be able to see how this activity can help you in your supervision duties. There is some overlap among the points that follow, but that is to be expected since they all arise from this one activity. Yet each is worthy of mention.

1.   *Observation statements need to be distinguished from other statements such as inferences, generalizations, and evaluations.* To observe is to use our senses to report what we experience. We use observation as an explanation of what has occurred, a foundation for future action, and as a reason for the actions we take. For example, if a police officer asks me why I was driving 55 mph on Highway X instead of 40 mph, I may answer, "I saw a sign which permitted me to resume my former speed of 55." Since I observed a sign posting the speed of 55 mph as legal, I increased my speed of 40 mph, which I had maintained while driving through a construction zone.

Since observations are a bedrock for legal decisions and since supervisory reports do have legal uses, it is necessary to be clear as to what is and what is not an observation. Keep in mind that a judge wants observations, not conclusions, from a witness. With this thought in mind, the following definitions will be helpful in distinguishing observation statements from other related statements:

Observe:	to perceive or pay attention to; to gather items of information through our senses; to acquire data through sense perceptions.
Infer:	to go beyond immediate observations and to construct patterns as a way of predicting future observations and of explaining events; to extend and interpret what is observed; to go beyond the information given; to conclude based on observations.
Generalize:	to condense large amounts of data into a statement that covers all items; some generalizations have predictive value (for example, all humans are mortal).
Evaluate:	to make a qualitative judgment; to rate in terms of good/bad, right/wrong, beautiful/ugly; to judge the value or worth of something; to opine; to offer a personal belief.
Recommend:	to suggest; to advise; to tell someone what to do; to direct the actions of someone regarding what should or ought to be done.

The above definitions are helpful but do not answer a critical question when trying to distinguish between an observation and an inference: "How can we draw the line between an observation and an inference?" For example, in the list in Figure 3-1 are Items 9 and 17 observations or inferences? Do we observe that the man portrayed is Abraham Lincoln or do we infer it? That is, do we observe only that the image is of a man or do we observe that it is Abraham Lincoln? Can we even claim that we observe a "man" or must we retreat further and say only that we observe the image of a human being? In short, what is an observation that is a result of our senses and what is an inference that goes beyond our senses and is based upon prior knowledge and interpretation?

The need to distinguish an observation from an inference is present when a supervisor confers with a teacher. Is the supervisor making an observation when he says, "You were angry at the students today." Is the comment on anger an observation or an inference? Is the supervisor reporting what occurred or is the supervisor interpreting the events that were observed? The difference, which at first may seem slight or even the result of hairsplitting, looms large, however, when supervisor and teacher seek to understand the complexities of classroom events, explain what occurred, and decide on future action to be taken.

Keep in mind the position taken by philosopher Robert Ennis. Ennis says that given that the purpose of observing is the securing of reliable knowledge, then the question about what is an observation becomes "In this field of inquiry, what sort of statement closely dependent on the senses can be relied on because of the likelihood of getting quick agreement among experienced people?"[1] That is to say, pragmatically the question is, "Is something likely to go wrong if we take this sort of statement as a starting point?"

When we apply the position of Ennis to the penny, then for a group of American teachers it is permissible to accept Item 9, Picture (image) of Abraham Lincoln, as an observation. We need not retreat to the more general statement, "There's an image of a man." However, if Item 9 were made in Albania, probably it would not be an observation but an inference—a conclusion—drawn from reflecting on all the information known about the penny. In Albania the observation would probably be, "There's a picture (image) of a man." The Albanians would not need to retreat to "There's an image of a human being." Similarly, the statement by the supervisor to a teacher, "You were angry at the students today," should be considered as an inference rather than an observation.

In short, it may be difficult sometimes to distinguish between the various statements that are made about a penny or teaching, especially between an observation statement and an inference statement. Nevertheless, it is worth the effort to make the necessary distinctions in order to facilitate communication, to establish the evidence which will count in an explanation of what has occurred, and to obtain agreement regarding a starting point for stating reasons for decisions about the future. Furthermore, in making the distinctions, we must remember that context is an important factor.

2. *Observing requires careful attention, time, and perhaps some device to enhance the capacity of our senses.* Although some people may consider the process of observing as an easy one, the truth is that observing, as with other processes and skills, requires practice and care in order to perform it correctly and adequately. Judges, lawyers, police officers, and witnesses know this well. When we observe, we use our senses, which are not always as sharp as we think they are or wish they would be. If we rush or if our senses are dulled for whatever reason, then the observations we make are less than complete and perhaps even inaccurate. Thus, with limited time we cannot observe everything, and with less than perfect senses combined with inexperience or a lack of recent honing of our skill it is fairly easy to err. This is especially true when we observe an event for which we have no record such as a photograph or video tape.

An event, in contrast to the static penny, is both dynamic and more complex. Hence, an ongoing event such as teaching is more likely to cause an observer difficulty than an object such as a penny, as in this activity. It is for this reason that it is quite helpful to use a tape recorder when observing because such a device allows the observer the opportunity to observe several times. As observer you can hear (and see if you use a video recording) the same section of the lesson more than one quick time. Still photographs of the lesson serve a similar purpose. Also, an observation guide allows you to channel your senses so that you enhance them by giving them clear direction. Just as the magnifying glass, ruler, or scale enhance the observations of the penny, the tape recorder, still camera, and observation guide enhance the observations of the teacher and students.

3. *To increase the power and range of our observations we should use as many of our five senses as possible.* Since observations are based on our senses, it is reasonable to claim that our observations gain strength when we use more than just one sense. In the observations listed in Figure 3-1, all but one, Item 24, stem from the sense of sight. Item 24 is a result of using the sense of touch. However, the senses of taste, smell, and hearing are not represented in the list. (On another occasion I did receive an observation based on hearing, "It sounds dull when you drop it on the table.") In any case, the participants in The Penny generally restrict their observations to those based on their sense of sight. Similarly, in regard to teaching, observers mainly use their sight and hearing without seeking ways, however restricted they may be, to observe through taste, smell, and touch. Although we might not be able to use more than our senses of sight and hearing in most cases, we do well to remember the other three senses and seek ways to use them. Furthermore, we do well to seek ways to enhance our capacity to observe through sight and hearing.

4. *It is easier to reach agreement among people about observations than about inferences and evaluations.* Observations, however difficult they may be to make, are generally more reliable than inferences and evaluations. In making observations, we use our sense perceptions to describe the world of objects and events around us. In making inferences and evaluations we build on observations and add our own interpretation and beliefs. For this reason inferences and evaluations are more complex and more likely to differ from one person to the next. Though three drama critics may observe the same Broadway play, they may disagree as to their inferences about the playwright's purpose and as to their judgments of the quality of the entire production.

5. *Reliability of observations can be increased.* The observations made by observers do not need to remain at the same level. If observers are not disposed to using an enhancement device, they can be taught how valuable such devices are and how to use them. Observers can learn to use new observation methods (or instruments, guidelines, checklists) and thereby increase the reliability and power of their observations. The act of practicing, aided by feedback, also serves to increase reliability of observations. For example, observers of the penny can learn a structured procedure which will guide them to thoroughness. They can learn to use a magnifying glass, a micrometer, a delicate scale, and chemical analysis techniques, all of which will enhance the observations they make. They can study about the art of coin design to increase their sensitivity to the use of busts, mottoes, architectural images, and symbols.

In like manner, as supervisors learn more about precise methods of observing and improve their skills in performance, they can and will earn a reputation for being thorough and neutral. They can learn to shed biases which skew observations. They can learn techniques for staying alert. As a result, with an earned reputation for being a skilled and competent observer a supervisor can increase the effectiveness of the communication which undergirds supervision.

SUGGESTIONS AND COMMENTS

1. Before doing this activity with your faculty, try it out with a few select friends just to get the hang of it. Try it as a social, parlor activity at your home. All you need is a minimum of four people to gain experience. Besides getting the feel of the activity, you will have a fun activity with your friends.

2. Practice making some distinctions yourself among statements so that you will be sensitive to a key point raised by this Penny activity. This practice will definitely help you lead the discussion based on the observations made by the participants.

3. Keep the magnifying glass, ruler, micrometer, and scale out of sight until you need them. If participants ask for one of these instruments, you can give it to them for their use. In my experience no one has ever asked for any enhancing instrument (though some already were using one in the form of eyeglasses or a hearing aid). When you do introduce the idea of an enhancing instrument and demonstrate what observations can be made with one, you will have the advantage of strengthening your point by a surprise move.

4. Decide in advance how you want to use your variant coins. You can, for example, reveal them one at a time during the discussion to show that pennies are different. You can show that with a scratched, messed up penny many of the observations made with a new coin would not be possible. Or, you can distribute one or two variants to the group at the very beginning in Step 1 so that all but one or two people have the same coin. For example, if everyone has a 1984 penny, you might slip one or two people a 1984-D penny. Then, you can watch to see the effect on the observations and on the group's reactions to the ensuing comments about the "D" or lack of it. Obviously, you can combine these two approaches by using some variants early and some later.

5. You can conduct the entire Penny activity in one hour. If you have more time, you can expand the listing of the observations on the chalkboard and the reviewing of each item of the longer list.

6. If for some reason you personally do not wish to lead this activity, by all means ask someone else to lead it. A staff member with a good background in making distinctions based on observations—perhaps a science or art background—would be an excellent choice to be leader. You can be a participant or observer, as you see fit.

APPLICATIONS

This structured Penny activity is not an end in itself. Its purpose is rather to serve as a sensitizing springboard for you in your work with your faculty. This activity will provide some key ideas and the realization that what appears as a common object can involve complex processes. In any case, you should build on the experience and discussion since the points apply to both teaching and supervision. Several suggestions follow:

REVIEW OF CURRENT OBSERVATION AND EVALUATION FORMS

You can easily use the ideas learned in The Penny as the basis for another look at your current observation and evaluation forms. You can examine what kinds of statements your forms lead your staff to make. For example, if you have a checklist of items on your observation form, you can examine the list to determine whether the observer *observes* the item or *infers* the item. You can ask whether the teacher receiving a completed form considers the form as a report of *observations* or *conclusions based on unspecified observations*.

Similarly, you can examine your evaluation form to determine the role observations and criteria play as foundations for the evaluations offered by the user of the form. For example, does the user specify the basic observations made that support the evaluations? Are the observations implied? Are the criteria explicit or implied? Are the criteria idiosyncratic to the user or are they publicly accepted throughout the entire school system?

You can suggest revisions of your forms that will sharpen them and thereby make their use more effective since those people who receive and read the forms will have a better sense of what the user is communicating. The revisions can be slight, yet they may serve to straighten out some inconsistencies and some ambiguities. Nevertheless, such revision can lead to greater acceptance by the receiver, the user, and subsequent reader on the Board of Education.

SPECIAL MEMO

One simple way to follow up on The Penny is to send a memo to your staff highlighting the points raised. Figure 3-2 is an easy one to use as a quick and effective method for informing your faculty about your views on the session. An example of a completed form is shown in Figure 3-3. Here the supervisor reminds the faculty that a committee has been established to review the supervision forms and update them in light of the points raised during the activity. Note that one of the key points listed refers to the process ("how") of observing rather than the object ("what") of observing. This is in contrast to what many supervision forms lead us to consider. That is to say, the forms generally lead us to think about what we will observe and are silent on how we will observe.

The purpose of the memo is twofold. First, it alerts the faculty to your view of the session by offering in concrete, written form what was discussed. Second, it serves as a springboard for faculty thinking. Each person will be reminded of the session and will be encouraged to rethink the points before a new session in which the faculty will be involved with the implementation of the ideas.

VIDEOTAPE PLAYBACK

Once the faculty is alert to the complexity of observing and the skill needed to do it well, you can graduate, so to speak, from a static penny to a videotape recording. You can ask one of the faculty members to prepare a brief tape recording for use with the staff. All you need is a short lesson since you will play it back in five- to ten-minute segments, in any case. (You may never play back more than two or three short sections in a playback session since the discussions arising from each section are time consuming). You can conduct the session with the videotape recording in a manner similar to the one suggested in the Penny activity.

TO: _____

FROM: _____

RE: Follow-up from The Penny

    Led by _____ on _____, 19___

1. Quotable quotes from the session:

    A.

    B.

    C.

2. Key points raised:

    A.

    B.

    C.

3. Decisions to follow through for implementation:

FIGURE 3-2. Follow-up memo for The Penny (blank).

TO: _____ All Supervisors _____

FROM: _____ Sal Pinolli _____

RE: Follow-up from The Penny

   Led by _____ Sal _____ on __March 10__ , 19__XX__

1. Quotable quotes from the session:

   A. I'm mad at myself for using only my eyes. (Erica)

   B. It's good we started out with a penny and not a lesson. (Gerry)

   C. Sal is a better hairsplitter than Lincoln was a rail-splitter. (Jeff)

2. Key points raised:

   A. The "how" of observing is as important as the "what."

   B. We agreed to tighten up our language as we loosen up our senses.

   C. Good observing is the basis for good evaluating.

3. Decisions to follow through for implementation:

   A committee of Jane, Jeff, and I will meet on March 17 to look over our district forms and propose revisions to use in our meeting scheduled for March 29. After our deliberations we'll send our suggestions to the Superintendent for consideration and possible approval by the teacher's group. To get the ball rolling send your personal suggestions to anyone on the committee by March 16.

FIGURE 3-3. Follow-up memo for The Penny (filled in).

CONCLUDING WORDS

The Penny is simple but sophisticated. It requires little material. The yield of this activity, however, is a realization that some of the skills we use daily in our personal and professional lives need resharpening if they are to serve us well. We can learn from the tennis players and violinists who practice often and warm up before they perform publicly. We are in constant need of maintaining our skills. If we do not maintain them, they become dull. The Penny activity leads us to recognize that for clarity in communication and for precision in supervision we need to make distinctions among the statements we make. With clarity and precision resulting from skilled observing, inferring, and evaluating we can be effective supervisors.

CHAPTER 3 ENDNOTE

1.   ROBERT H. ENNIS, *Logic in Teaching* (Englewood Cliffs, N.J.: Prentice-Hall, Inc., 1969).

4

THE PRISONER'S

DILEMMA

Trust and Group Benefit

The Prisoner's Dilemma presents an age-old situation where two people must act separately while realizing that what each decides will directly affect the life of the other person. Can and will each prisoner trust the other person to act in a way that will help them both? Or, will each act in a way that elevates immediate self-interest above a concern for the other person? In short, what is the value and effect of trust for two people who must respond to an interrogator about a reported crime? From their experience in this structured activity, participants will be able to discuss the value of trust, the results of face-to-face communication, and the long-run advantage of acting according to the concept of group benefit.

After reading this chapter, you should be able to:

- Understand the purpose of, steps for, and points raised by The Prisoner's Dilemma.
- Conduct The Prisoner's Dilemma activity confidently with your faculty following the step-by-step strategy presented.
- Describe at least five points generally raised in the debriefing discussion.
- Distinguish points raised that relate to the social dynamics of the activity from those that relate to the specific legal scenario.
- Know how to apply the points raised by this structured activity in two different ways.

OVERVIEW

The Prisoner's Dilemma activity offers you the opportunity to inquire into mutual trust, fairness, self-interest, social benefit, face-to-face communication, and anger arising from the breaking of trust. This activity offers a somewhat rare and excellent opportunity to examine anger and disappointment, emotions which result when people who expect trust from others realize that trust has been cast aside for self-interest. Participants simulate pairs of prisoners in jail who are arrested and asked to confess to a crime. They record their responses and their impressions of each other. The debriefing examines how the prisoners responded to the request for confession, the interaction between prisoners, the feelings aroused by the interaction, and the values which underpin the scenario and procedures.

MATERIALS NEEDED

For each participant you will need: a Record Sheet (see Figure 4-1); a copy of the Scenario Sheet (see Figure 4-2), which contains the Situation, the Summary of Probable Penalties, and the Payoff Chart; and a blank piece of paper. Each participant will also need a pencil or pen. It is best to conduct this activity in a room that allows you the ability to move the participants' chairs to allow them to sit back-to-back or face-to-face as the activity proceeds. (See Step 10 under "Procedure"; if you decide to distribute a new Record Sheet rather than extend the old one, you will need two copies of the Record Sheet for each participant.)

NUMBER OF PARTICIPANTS

You can conduct this activity with any number of participants from four to 100 though, of course, the debrief discussion will be somewhat difficult with any more than thirty and less than six. A group of ten to twenty people yields five to ten pairs of people, thus providing for a desirable variation in responses. You should seek to involve everyone as a participant. Since participants work in pairs, there can be at most only one person uninvolved as a prisoner at any given time. (See Step 3 under "Procedure" for dealing with this situation.)

PROCEDURE

Step 1. Warm up the group by simply telling them that this activity deals with prisoners. As yet, do not provide information about the scenario, rules, or objectives. It is important that you get everyone into the activity quickly. Participants need the opportunity to discover the meaning of their actions for themselves.

Step 2. Distribute the Scenario Sheet (see Figure 4-2). Go over the situation with the group so that everyone understands it. You can check understanding and explain the scenario in alternate ways by using the summary of probable penalties and the payoff chart. Be sure to review the penalties for each of the four possible combinations of decisions for the two participants involved:

Prisoner A	not confess
Prisoner B	not confess

Prisoner A	not confess
Prisoner B	confess

Prisoner A	confess
Prisoner B	not confess

Prisoner A	confess
Prisoner B	confess

Do not get bogged down here. Be clear and move on. Clarity will come as the activity progresses.

	My Choice	Other's Choice	My Penalty	Other's Penalty
1				
2				
3				
4				
5				
6				
7				
8				
9				
10				

FIGURE 4-1. Record sheet for The Prisoner's Dilemma (blank).

SITUATION

A police officer stops a car with a driver and passenger for speeding just minutes after learning of an armed robbery in the neighborhood. The police officer notices the handle of a revolver sticking out of the belt of each person. The officer asks to see their permits to carry the guns. When they fail to produce the permits, the police officer arrests them and brings them back to the police station for booking and questioning.

At the station a detective separates the two people and notifies them of their constitutional rights. The detective suspects but cannot prove that they are involved in the armed robbery and gives them the choice to confess or not to confess to the crime. The detective tells them if they both confess to the armed robbery and plead guilty, then the police will ask the prosecutor to recommend to the judge that they receive a prison term of 2-3 years each, which is less than the maximum sentence. Also, if one person confesses and pleads guilty and one does not, then the confessor will probably be able to work out a plea bargain for lenient treatment, which will limit the sentence to 6-12 months in return for turning state's evidence while the police will "slap the book" at the nonconfessor for a sentence of 3-5 years. Both persons realize that if neither of them confesses, the detective probably will not be able to prove them guilty of armed robbery and will book them for illegal possession of weapons, for which they each will get a relatively moderate punishment, 18 months each.

Neither person is aware of the other's decision. The decision of each will be very much affected by the prediction of what the other will decide.

SUMMARY OF PROBABLE PENALTIES
AFTER CONVICTION—TIME IN JAIL

If both prisoners do not confess, they each get 18 months.

If both prisoners confess, they each get 2–3 years.

If one prisoner confesses and turns state's evidence and one does not, then the confessor gets 6–12 months and the nonconfessor gets 3–5 years.

PAYOFF CHART: TIME IN JAIL

| | | PRISONER A | |
		NOT CONFESS	CONFESS
PRISONER B	NOT CONFESS	18 MONTHS EACH	6-12 MONTHS – A 3-5 YEARS – B
	CONFESS	3-5 YEARS – A 6-12 MONTHS – B	2-3 YEARS EACH

FIGURE 4-2. Scenario sheet for The Prisoner's Dilemma.

Step 3.   Designate one person as your reserve person. This participant should be the person who could, if need be, serve as official activity observer. Right now just ask that person to step aside.

Step 4.   Ask the remaining participants to pair off and sit back-to-back. Pairs should move their chairs around so that they sit comfortably back-to-back. If there is a participant left over, then your reserve person pairs up with that person. If there is no one left over, then publicly designate your reserve person as official activity observer.

Step 5.   Announce *the rules to the prisoners*:

1. No talking or writing to each other until explicitly permitted by leader (yourself) of this activity.
2. Each person privately decides to confess or not to confess. Each person writes the decision on a piece of paper. Each person writes only "Confess" or "Not Confess."
3. The goal of this activity is "Do the best you can." (State the goal this way. Say this and nothing more.)

Step 6.   Ask the prisoners, who are sitting silently back-to-back, to make their decisions. Each prisoner should write a decision on the top of the blank piece of paper and pass that paper over his or her shoulder to the other prisoner. Remind the prisoners not to talk to each other.

Step 7.   Distribute the Record Sheet (see Figure 4-2) now. Ask the prisoners to fill in the *first row*. Check to see that everyone understands how to fill in the Record Sheet correctly. (A sample correct Record Sheet appears in Figure 4-3. Note that in ten turns only two of the four possible combinations of decisions appear.)

Step 8.   Ask the prisoners to continue the same process nine more times for a total of ten turns. Clearly announce that each prisoner may decide to confess or not to confess during each turn independently of any previous decision. That is, each turn involves a

	My Choice	Other's Choice	My Penalty	Other's Penalty
1	NoT CONFESS	CONFESS	3-5 YEARS	6-12 MONTHS
2	" "	"	" "	" "
3	" "	"	" "	" "
4	CONFESS	"	2-3 "	2-3 YEARS
5	"	"	" "	" "
6	NOT CONFESS	"	3-5 "	6-12 MONTHS
7	" "	"	" "	" "
8	" "	"	" "	" "
9	" "	"	" "	" "
10	CONFESS	"	2-3 "	2-3 YEARS

FIGURE 4-3. Record sheet for The Prisoner's Dilemma (filled in).

separate and independent decision. Remind the group that the pattern is: write decision; pass paper with decision; record decisions and penalties.

Step 9.   When *all* prisoners have finished ten complete turns, ask the pairs to face each other and talk together for three to five minutes. Direct each pair in this face-to-face situation to talk about what happened during the ten turns based on the Scenario Sheet and the *completed* Record Sheet.

Step 10.   After three to five minutes, ask the pairs to sit back-to-back once again, not to talk to each other, and to repeat the pattern of deciding-passing-recording another ten turns—a grand total of twenty times. Remind them to write-pass-record *one turn at a time*. Ask them not to talk to each other when they have completed their twentieth turn. You may distribute a new Record Sheet to everyone or ask prisoners to extend the old one on their own. (See Figure 4-4 for a sample completed Record Sheet after twenty turns.)

	My Choice	Other's Choice	My Penalty	Other's Penalty
1	NOT CONFESS	CONFESS	3-5 YEARS	6-12 MONTHS
2	" "	"	" "	" "
3	" "	"	" "	" "
4	CONFESS	"	2-3 YEARS	2-3 YEARS
5	"	"	" "	" "
6	NOT CONFESS	"	3-5 "	6-12 MONTHS
7	" "	"	" "	" "
8	" "	"	" "	" "
9	" "	"	" "	" "
10	CONFESS	"	2-3 "	2-3 YEARS
11	NOT CONFESS	NOT CONFESS	18 MONTHS	18 MONTHS
12	" "	" "	" "	" "
13	" "	" "	" "	" "
14	" "	" "	" "	" "
15	" "	" "	" "	" "
16	" "	" "	" "	" "
17	" "	" "	" "	" "
18	" "	" "	" "	" "
19	" "	" "	" "	" "
20	" "	CONFESS	3-5 YEARS	6-12 MONTHS

FIGURE 4-4. Record sheet for The Prisoner's Dilemma (filled in).

Step 11.   When *all* the prisoners have completed the twentieth turn, ask each prisoner to write on a piece of paper at least three words or phrases to describe his or her impression of the other prisoner. Each prisoner should consider only what is known from this activity and should discount everything known about that person prior to this activity. In other words, each prisoner will be completing the sentence, "The other prisoner was _____," at least three times while still sitting back-to-back and before any more talking begins. Here is a sampling of terms and phrases previously used by participants:

Consistent	Sneaky	Altruistic	Trustworthy
Reasonable	Stubborn	Undecided	Understanding
Trusting	Illogical	Predictable	Easy to talk to
Honest	Determined	Practical	Not a person I'd rob
Logical	Supportive	Convinced of innocence	a bank with
Concerned	Dishonest	Brave	Not to be trusted
Loyal	Sincere	Out for himself	

Step 12.   When all prisoners have finished writing their three terms, ask them to face each other again, exchange papers, and talk together about their experience since their last conference.

Step 13.   Begin debriefing after a few minutes. As you debrief, try to keep your role as discussion facilitator and paraphraser. Try not to "preach" to the group. Patience will pay off.

Read through the section entitled "Points Raised by Activity" to alert yourself to the points that generally come out during this discussion. Do not try to force more points than the group is willing to initiate because the forced points probably will not be meaningful anyway. Keep the extra points in mind, note them, and use some other activities in this book to help bring them to your faculty.

Notice that there are many sample questions below. You will no doubt not need to ask every question since many of the points will come to the floor without your solicitation. Ask only those questions you want to ask and need to ask in order to keep the discussion going.

Follow the debriefing strategy below so you can reap the benefits of this structured activity:

1. Shift into the debriefing session by simply and only saying something like, "Now, let's talk about what happened so far."

2. Begin the discussion by encouraging the participants to *describe what happened*. Let them "ventilate." Without sufficient hard-fact ventilation, there will not be an adequate basis for making discoveries and drawing conclusions later on. This opening phase of the debriefing will loosen up the participants and get them talking, as it is very easy to talk on this concrete, nonthreatening level. *Be sure to call on the official activity observer, if you had one, to give a report.* Ask such questions as: What decisions did you make, confess or not confess? Who remained silent and did not talk at all to the police? Who demanded to see a lawyer before talking to the police? Who switched

decisions somewhere during the twenty turns? Could you and did you predict the other prisoner's decisions after a while? What did you talk about during the three- to five-minute conversation after the tenth turn? What terms and phrases did you use to describe the other prisoner? What did the instruction "Do the best you can" mean to you? What made you feel good during the activity? What made you feel bad during the activity?

3. *Analyze the meaning (purpose, points, or messages) of this activity.* Discuss what all of the action adds up to—what the point of the activity is. Ask such questions as: What does all this mean to you? What key ideas does this activity present to us? What did you learn about yourself and others from participating in this activity? What do the results teach us? What does this activity teach us about trusting another person? What was the effect of face-to-face communication? What does sitting back-to-back represent in regard to communicating with another person? What do the written notes mean as compared with the face-to-face conference? How did you develop trust, if you did? What prevented you from developing trust, if you didn't develop it? Were you better off considering and looking out for yourself or seeking the cooperation of the other person? Does self-interest at the expense of the other person or group interest with everyone in mind pay off better in the long run?

4. *Examine the implications of this activity for teaching and supervision.* Ask such questions as: Are there parallels between this activity and teaching? Are there parallels between this activity and supervision? What applications do you see for us based on all these points? In what ways can we change our classroom activities as a result of what we have learned from participating in this structured activity? In what ways can we modify our supervision procedures as a result of what we have learned from participating in this structured activity?

5. *Summarize, generalize, and conclude.* Tie the many points together—the messages, the parallels, and the implications. Do not assume that the participants will generalize and draw conclusions on their own without guidance. Ask such questions as: From all we have said and done, what conclusions do you draw from this activity? What can you say to summarize what we have said today?

If you wish, you can do the summarizing in a different way. You can request the group to list some key ideas that have come forth during the discussion and to offer some generalizations based on these key ideas. This approach is effective since the generalizations grow immediately and directly from what the group says. You can initiate this approach by asking each person to complete whichever of the following sentence stems you feel is more appropriate:

Based on this activity, I realize about teaching that

_____

Based on this activity, I realize about supervising that

_____

Be sure to ask the group to read their completed sentences.

Step 14.   Move forward. Before leaving The Prisoner's Dilemma behind, structure the situation so that you launch yourself and the group into something new built on it. In this way, you bridge current activity with future activity while interest is high. For example, you might prepare a brainstorming session where faculty could list specific ways they believe a sense of trust could be bolstered in the group. Suggest that you will provide a summary of this activity just to get the next session off to a good start. (See "Applications" for additional ideas.)

POINTS RAISED BY ACTIVITY

It may be difficult for you as you read through this description of The Prisoner's Dilemma to realize just what people will say during the conferences after the tenth and twentieth turns and during the debriefing discussion. To help you, below are twelve points *related to teaching and supervising* that generally come up during this activity. You may find some others as well. By familiarizing yourself with these points you will know what to expect and also be able to see how this activity can help you in your supervision duties. There is some overlap among the points that follow, but that is to be expected since they all arise from this one activity. Yet each is worthy of mention.

1. *Mutual trust arises when people work together to solve a common problem.* People do not often trust each other when they begin interacting. Though we might like to start off with the ability to rely on someone we don't know or don't know well, we are somewhat wary of people when we begin working together. For whatever reason that we are wary and choose to hold back our full commitment and trust, we must recognize that most often the lack of trust exists when people begin interacting. While we do not generally mistrust 100 percent, we also do not trust 100 percent. We develop mutual trust as our interaction continues and as we come to know each other through common experiences. We probably cannot point to any single, big event that leads to mutual trust. Rather, a sense of trust evolves from a series of small events in which we realize that the other person cares and will act in our best interests. The development of trust takes time, effort, and common experiences.

The importance of trust between people who must interact and think about each other even when not together is seen in the many terms and phrases used by "prisoners" to describe each other. Whether stated in the positive or the negative, the concept of trust is present in the impressions prisoners have of each other. Since each person's fate depends on the other's actions, the need for trust is present and strong, of course.

2. *Face-to-face communication is desirable and promotes the development of trust and mutual benefit.* It is better for people who share a common problem to communicate with each other face-to-face than to communicate through written notes (back-to-back) or through some intermediary. Even a few minutes of direct, face-to-face communication can promote trust in a way that indirect communication never can. This is so because of the many nonverbal messages we communicate to other people as we talk together directly. Participants in The Prisoner's Dilemma often point to the three- to five-minute conference after the tenth turn as being most effective in allowing them to establish ways to cope with their dilemma effectively.

3. *Group benefit does not necessarily arise in a group when people pursue their own self-interests.* In our society some people advocate that individuals should seek their self-interest and thereby help to promote the common good. This position is acceptable until one person's self-interest works to the detriment of a second person. Although some people may think that the accumulation of all the separate self-interest actions will lead to group benefit, the opposite is true. When what is best for one person yields a bad result for another and vice versa, the actions they take toward the goals of individual self-interest obviously do not lead to maximum group benefit.

A different concept, group benefit (social benefit or mutual benefit), must replace self-interest. Indeed, people need to realize that in the long run they do better when they consider the context and general consequences of their actions. Such is the case in a family, neighborhood, school, or any other group. The people in a group are better off when they work together, respect each other, perform their individual functions well, and promote the welfare of each person and the group. If you wish to see how this actually works in the use of natural resources by a group of people, see the excellent collection of essays edited by Garret Hardin and John Baden.[1]

We see this in the payoff chart penalties, which correctly reflect the general legal state today. If Prisoner A thinks only of himself, he will confess because he hopes to get only a six-month sentence while Prisoner B serves three to five years. If Prisoner B thinks only of herself, she will confess because she hopes to get only a six-month sentence while Prisoner A serves three to five years. The result of such thinking about self-interest is that both prisoners serve two to three years. If they trust each other and consider their mutual benefit, they will each serve only eighteen months. It is this line of consideration that leads to the next point, but first a pertinent limerick:

> *There once were two cats of Kilkenny*
> *Each thought there was one cat too many*
> *So they scratched and they bit*
> *And they fought and they fit*
> *Till instead of two cats there weren't any.*

4. *If a person breaks a cooperative agreement with another person or violates an established feeling of mutual trust, the hurt person feels angry and often is vindictive.* The breaking of an agreement to cooperate or the violation of a trusting relationship that has developed over a period of time is a serious offense in the eyes of the hurt person. The anger that the hurt person feels is evident and difficult to remove. It is more serious than the anger one feels, for example, about losing a watch or wallet to a pickpocket. The anger over a loss of property is not nearly as deep and stinging as the anger over the loss of trust. Though the hurt person may not consciously act negatively in return, there may well be some vindictiveness. Such is the way people behave. It is for this reason that when a "prisoner" in this structured activity feels "zapped" by the other person, there is anger expressed in the terms used after the twentieth turn. We see this "zapping" in Figure 4-4. For nine turns after their face-to-face conference Prisoner A and Prisoner B decided to "Not Confess." This decision probably arose from their understanding of the situation as they talked over the first ten turns. However, one prisoner on the twentieth turn broke the agreement and trust which emerged after the tenth turn. Thus, at the end of the twentieth turn one prisoner is serving three to five years while the other is serving a much lighter sentence of six to twelve months. It is this situation that accounts for such negative terms and phrases as "out for himself," "sneaky," and "not to be trusted."

Experience from many debriefings show that the "zapped" or hurt person feels quite angry and expresses the anger openly.

5. *People have different interpretations of the same directive.* Although each person in a group may hear the same words of a speech or witness the same event, even a fairly simple one, there will be several different interpretations as to the meaning of that speech or event. While the board of education may issue a policy statement about goals for the schools that reaches each faculty member via a written statement, there immediately arise several different interpretations as to the "real intent" or "true meaning" of the policy. In this structured activity the same situation arises when participants act upon the directive given by the leader in Step 5 of the "Procedure": "Do the best you can." There are differences of interpretation about the words "best" and "you" that lead to different actions during the activity.

6. *When people are emotionally charged up, they often do not act in a logical, reasonable way.* The excitement of the emotions, whether they are anger, love, jealousy, fear, or a combination of them, leads to behavior which is often not desirable when judged from a logical point of view. The arousal of strong emotions somehow blocks our capacity for logical, reasonable thinking. When we are in serious fear, for example, we may panic and act in a way which actually is counter to our best interests. Similarly, if we become angry and vindictive, we may concentrate so much on "getting even" with the source of our trouble that we overreact. Our anger may get the best of us and inhibit straight thinking. Such is the position of the "prisoner" who is "zapped" and can think only of revenge in the short run.

7. *When people understand their situations themselves and the probable consequences of their actions, conditions are favorable for change to occur.* It is difficult for people to plan for change and to seek change when they don't know what consequences to expect from their actions. It is also difficult for people to plan for change when they don't have a good grasp on what is the nature of their actions. That is, people need to know as fully as possible what the current situation is. They need feedback about what is happening now as well as knowledge about probable consequences of current and future actions.

In this structured activity the prisoners can and do plan for the future because they understand the current situation and are clear about future penalties. With knowledge available to them, the prisoners can plan and change their actions. Change is not frightening because they have a grasp on the situation at hand.

8. There is a group of points that relates to the specific scenario dealing with the prisoners from the armed robbery. These messages concern the law and are not generally applicable to supervision. Yet, participants like to discuss these points because they pertain to their daily lives as citizens in a democracy. When using this structured activity to discuss the supervisory or teaching relationship, it is best to downplay the following points in favor of the seven above. However, if you or one of your teachers wishes to discuss the American legal system in a social studies class, for example, then the following points will no doubt come forth as the most important ones. Therefore, the "scenario points" below are offered to you in case you use this activity for another purpose, for which it is well suited also. The five points appear without commentary or explanation.

a.   A person often can obtain a reduced sentence through plea bargaining.

b.   The police by law must notify a person, prior to questioning, of his Constitutional (Fifth Amendment) rights: (1) the person has an absolute right to remain silent; (2) any statement the person makes may be used as evidence against him at trial in a court of law; (3) the person has a right to the assistance of an attorney; and (4) if the person cannot afford his own attorney, then the court will appoint one to provide counsel free of charge. These are the so-called Miranda warnings or Miranda rights based on the decision in Miranda v. Arizona, 384 U.S. 436 (1966).

c.   A police officer can take a person to the police station for booking and further questioning when the officer makes an arrest.

d.   A detective cannot promise the suspects a reduced sentence for cooperation. The detective can only recommend to the prosecutor that the latter attempt to obtain a lighter sentence.

e.   Carrying a gun without a permit is illegal.

SUGGESTIONS AND COMMENTS

1.   As with the other structured activities, it is wise to try out The Prisoner's Dilemma with a few select friends in order to become familiar with it. The practice session will acquaint you with the strategy for conducting the activity as well as the points people focus on during the debriefing. You will gain some experience directing attention to the points pertinent to supervision that can aid you in your work with your faculty.

2.   Be sure to leave plenty of time for the debriefing. Since there are many points which the participants can and will raise about their experiences as prisoners who faced the classic dilemma, you will not be able to stop the participants easily once they begin to talk. Therefore, move the writing-passing-recording phase of the activity along at a brisk pace if necessary. You can conduct the entire activity in about an hour and a quarter if you proceed briskly.

3.   Do not short-circuit the activity by cutting down the number of turns the prisoners have to write-pass-record. The prisoners need time and opportunities to develop trust. If you are trying to save time, do so by shortening the warm-up time at the beginning of the activity. If you shorten the activity too much, the desired effects will not result. So, be careful with your timing.

4.   Be alert to the fact that participants will raise many issues, especially relating to plea bargaining and the Miranda warnings. You can relate these to your supervision situation if you wish or treat them lightly as you turn to points that are not focused so specifically on the law but rather on the social relationship between the prisoners. That is, keep in mind the difference between Points 1 to 7 and the five items mentioned in Point 8 under "Points Raised by Activity."

5.   If you personally do not feel comfortable leading this activity, by all means ask someone else to lead it. Perhaps, a person expert in social communication would be an excellent leader on your behalf. You can be a participant or observer, as you see fit.

APPLICATIONS

This structured activity is obviously not an end in itself. It is but one way for you to provide your faculty with an opportunity to discuss some points relevant to teaching and supervising that can help you in your work. The activity provides the opportunity to talk about group benefit, for example, and the shortsightedness of self-interest in a faculty which must work together to provide a good educational program for students. You can direct your group's attention to classroom applications if you are working with teachers or to supervisory applications if you are working with supervisors. In either case, you can easily apply the points raised by this structured activity.

SPECIAL MEMO

One simple way to push forward is to follow up the activity by sending a memo to each participant highlighting some particular points raised during the debriefing session. Figure 4-5 is an easy one to use for the highlighting purpose. An example of a completed form appears in Figure 4-6. Here the supervisor, an assistant superintendent for curriculum and instruction, focuses on the need for more personal (face-to-face) conferences as a means of establishing trust among supervisors from the central office and teachers in the various schools in the district. Her aim is brief and clear: more personal conferences with the teachers.

This special memo serves to recall to all the participants their experiences at the activity session. Second, it serves as an opportunity for you to show your impressions of the activity session and what you thought was the overall message conveyed to everyone. It allows you to focus the group's attention again by briefly selecting key quotations and points. As such it prepares your group for the next session so you can have another beneficial meeting.

INDIVIDUAL CONFERENCES

Since the theme of this structured activity is the value of face-to-face conferences and mutual trust, it is appropriate for you to schedule brief conferences with the people you supervise. You can meet with one or two people at a time. The session should be brief—ten to twenty minutes perhaps—to demonstrate that a conference can be brief but effective. Furthermore, it is important that you work towards finding a common problem to solve or project to work on where each of you can contribute in some way. That is to say, each of you should leave the conference with something achievable within a short amount of time. This will provide a further opportunity to show that you two or three can work together in a trusting way.

TO: _____

FROM: _____

RE: Follow-up from The Prisoner's Dilemma

    Led by _____ on _____, 19___

1. Quotable quotes from the session:

    A.

    B.

    C.

2. Key points raised:

    A.

    B.

    C.

3. Decisions to follow through for implementation:

FIGURE 4-5. Follow-up memo for The Prisoner's Dilemma (blank).

TO: Faculty, Elem. & Middle Schools

FROM: Sarabeth Miller, Assistant Superintendent

RE: Follow-up from the Prisoner's Dilemma

Led by   Jack Newcomer   on   Aug. 28   , 19XX

1. Quotable quotes from the session:

   A. Mike: I'll never rob a bank with Tony; he's concerned only in saving his own hide.

   B. Stephanie: There's no such thing as self-interest that doesn't consider the whole situation. If you're really interested in self-interest, you must make sure you don't do in your friends around you.

2. Key points raised:

   A. If you want to be trusted, you should trust the other person.

   B. A five-minute personal conference is more effective than a month's worth of written exchanges.

   C. Trust is easier to develop when you confer face-to-face than when you hide behind a piece of paper.

3. Decisions to follow through for implementation:

   Review our procedures to see if we can facilitate brief personal conference.

FIGURE 4-6. Follow-up memo for The Prisoner's Dilemma (filled in).

CONCLUDING WORDS

The Prisoner's Dilemma is a classic statement of the dilemma people face in their lives: on the one hand, people care about themselves first and seek their own self-interest sometimes even at the expense of someone else; on the other hand, people must consider others even if it means that their own personal benefit (at least in the short run) will be less than when they value their self-interest. The Prisoner's Dilemma scenario is one that is used by researchers investigating how people work together. It is also an excellent vehicle for supervisors who seek to explore the effects of face-to-face communication and the development of trust among people who work together in a school system. The theme of trust is a significant one for supervision because without trust there can be little worthwhile meaning in supervision at all levels.

CHAPTER 4 ENDNOTE

1. GARRETT HARDIN and JOHN BADEN, eds., *Managing the Commons* (San Francisco: W. H. Freeman, 1977).

5

THE SUPERVISION WINDOW

Awareness and Openness

What do you see when you look into a mirror? Yourself, of course. What do you see when you look into and through The Supervision Window? Yourself and a teacher you supervise. With The Supervision Window, you see yourself and someone else in supervisory interaction. You are known to others in a way that influences how those people react to and understand you. On the other hand, what you know about others influences how you react to and understand them. Indeed, through some abstract level of communication you may come to understand a teacher in a way that the teacher him- or herself does not even know. This is because, as you interact with your teachers, you communicate on several levels at the same time to foster an awareness that goes beyond explicit verbal messages.

The Supervision Window, which is a changing view of interaction, offers you the opportunity to explore the theme of awareness and openness in supervision. This theme is significant because, in order to develop professionally, teachers and supervisors need to be aware of what is occurring in their environment and to be open to change.

After reading this chapter, you should be able to:

- Understand the theoretical basis of The Supervision Window and the points raised when its internal dimensions are varied through supervisory interaction.
- Explain The Supervision Window's theoretical structure, including the four quadrants.
- Conduct The Supervision Window confidently with your faculty and colleagues following the step-by-step strategy.
- Understand and describe at least five points that are generally raised by participants.
- Suggest at least two ways you can apply the points in the debriefing discussion to your supervision procedures.

OVERVIEW

Based on The Johari Window developed by Joseph Luft[1] and Harry Ingham in 1955, The Supervision Window's participants—teachers and/or supervisors—begin to look at themselves as they know other people and as they are known by others. The participants establish a theoretical position, a model of a beginning position in supervision, and a model of their goal in supervision. Then the participants vary the dimensions of what is known and what is unknown between them. In doing so they become aware of how the actions they take affect other people. The debriefing discussion focuses on the points gained by each person in this interactive activity involving awareness and openness.

MATERIALS NEEDED

You will need copies of Figures 5-1, 5-2, 5-3, 5-6, and 5-9; paper; and a box of flat toothpicks.

NUMBER OF PARTICIPANTS

There is no limit to the number of people who can participate in this activity at the same time. You should have at least two people—a teacher and a supervisor—to vary the window areas and to talk over the variations. However, for a debriefing that delves into several areas, raises a variety of points, and allows people to hear other viewpoints on an issue, you should have at least five people, including yourself, to exchange ideas.

PROCEDURE

Step 1. Introduce this activity *very briefly*. Simply ask the group to join you in an activity that you believe is beneficial to all of you, as will be evident in the ensuing discussion. Be sure not to reveal what will happen. The idea is for the group to realize on its own what has happened when they debrief in Step 8. So, say little and be brief in order to get the activity going quickly.

Step 2. Distribute copies of Figure 5-1 to each participant. Use the figure to *explain the fundamental ideas* of The Supervision Window as follows. This figure is designed to emphasize the concept of awareness in the interpersonal relationship between the teacher and the supervisor. That is, from the teacher's point of view, there are ideas, feelings, behaviors, beliefs, and skills that the teacher knows and doesn't know about himself. These ideas may be known or unknown to the supervisor. In this way, there are four combinations of known and unknown ideas, feelings, behaviors, beliefs, and skills.

The four combinations become the four quadrants (or areas or panes) of the window. Quadrant 1 is labeled "Public." (Some people call this the "open" or "shared" quadrant.) The Public quadrant includes those things known both to the teacher and to the supervisor about the teacher. This is shared knowledge and both teacher and

	Known to Teacher	Unknown to Teacher
Known to **Supervisor**	1 PUBLIC	2 BLIND
Unknown to **Supervisor**	3 PRIVATE	4 UNPERCEIVED

The labels of the quadrants are from the teacher's perspective.

FIGURE 5-1. Labels of quadrants for The Supervision Window.

supervisor are aware of it. For example, the teacher is absent and called in sick. The teacher knows that he is truly absent due to the flu and the supervisor knows this also because the teacher left school yesterday with chills and a fever.

Quadrant 2 is labeled "Blind." (Some people call it the "bad breath" quadrant.) Here the supervisor knows something about the teacher that the teacher isn't aware of himself. Often the blind aspect of our behavior results from nonverbal messages that we communicate but that we are not aware of ourselves. The teacher, for example, may exhibit a pattern of behavior such as seating the girls to his right and the boys to his left, away from the windows, and may not be aware of it at all. Yet, the supervisor during the observation visit may notice the seating arrangement almost immediately. In regard to the preference in seating, the teacher has a personal blind spot known to the supervisor.

Quadrant 3 is labeled "Private." (Some people call it the "concealed," "secret," or "hidden" quadrant.) Here the teacher knows things about himself as teacher that the supervisor does not know. There is not shared knowledge about the teacher but one-way knowledge, which for whatever reason, the teacher only knows. It may include items that the teacher deliberately does not reveal as well as items that simply do not become Public because the supervisor and teacher do not interact much. For example, the teacher may realize that he has trouble working with three particular students in algebra.

However, he does not initiate a conference about the situation and the supervisor does not observe the classroom often enough to notice the situation either. This knowledge remains "Private" for the teacher.

Quadrant 4 is labeled "Unperceived." (Some people call this the "unknown" quadrant.) This quadrant includes things about the teacher which are as yet unperceived by both the teacher and supervisor alike. Though it may seem strange at first to believe, it is no doubt true that there are things about the teacher which neither the teacher or supervisor perceive now. The supervisor may not perceive them simply because of lack of familiarity and closeness with the teacher. The teacher may not perceive them because they are unconscious, nonverbal behaviors. It may well be that students, however, do perceive some of these things. For example, the teacher may be acting unfairly to the girls in geometry. The teacher, unaware of holding very low expectations in mathematics for girls, may be grading homework and tests tougher for girls than for boys. The supervisor may not know this because of a lack of a careful review of teacher-scored homework and tests and because the observation visits are focused on teacher questioning patterns. Nevertheless, the girl students may well recognize this unfairness of the teacher based upon a societal belief, which unfortunately is not disappearing fast enough, that girls in general simply are not as good in higher math as boys.

Step 3.   If necessary, *briefly* clarify any points about the theoretical model of the four quadrants based on the concept of awareness. Keep this brief because most points will clarify themselves as the activity continues with the participants varying the quadrants. Base your brief clarification on the points raised below.

Step 4.   Distribute copies of Figures 5-2 and 5-3 and four flat toothpicks to each participant. Ask each person to place the four toothpicks on Figure 5-3 as shown in Figure 5-4.

In this way, the four toothpicks will form a manipulable model of The Supervision Window. This particular formation will resemble the theoretical model of Figure 5-1. With an analogy to a clock, the four toothpicks are called: twelve o'clock line (because it passes through the twelve on the clock), the three o'clock line, the six o'clock line, and the nine o'clock line.

Step 5.   Ask the participants to look at Figure 5-2. The worksheet asks the participants to vary the dimensions of the four quadrants by moving the four toothpicks either to the right, left, up, or down. That is, slide the toothpick in the direction indicated without rotating it; do not change its angle relative to the other toothpicks. Ask people to work individually, in pairs, or in trios (as *you* prefer) and to move the toothpicks according to Column 2. Ask them to fill in Columns 3 and 4 as they proceed down the form. In thinking about the change they see each time occurring in The Supervision Window, they should fill in Column 5 briefly with possible causes for the new situation. After they finish with each of the eight variations, they should place the toothpick that was moved back to its original position. For example, Item 1 directs participants to move the twelve o'clock line to the right. When they do so, the formation shown in Figure 5-5 results.

Figure 5-6 shows how the first line on the worksheet shown in Figure 5-2 would look.

In other words, Figure 5-6 shows that the Public area expands as the Blind area shrinks due to the communication by the supervisor to the teacher of what was observed

1	2	3	4	5
Line	Move In Direction*	Area That Expands	Area That Shrinks	Cause
1 12 o'clock	Right			
2 9 o'clock	Up			
3 9 o'clock	Down			
4 6 o'clock	Right			
5 12 o'clock	Left			
6 3 o'clock	Down			
7 3 o'clock	Up			
8 6 o'clock	Left			

*Before moving the next line, be sure to replace the previous line in its original position.

FIGURE 5-2. Worksheet for The Supervision Window.

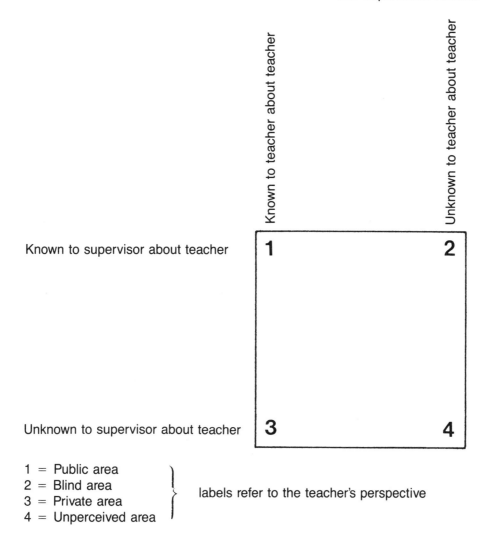

FIGURE 5-3. Workplate for The Supervision Window.

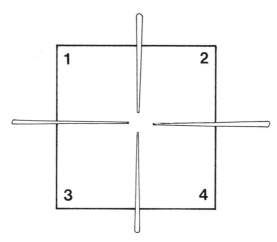

FIGURE 5-4. Arrangement of toothpicks for The Supervision Window.

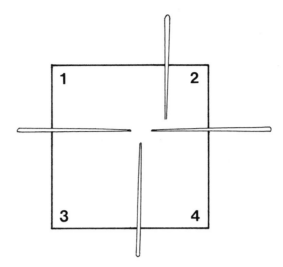

FIGURE 5-5. Position of toothpicks after moving the twelve o'clock line of The Supervision Window.

during a visit to the classroom. The "cause" suggested in Column 5 of Figure 5-6 is but one possible cause to explain why Public expands and Blind shrinks.

Remind the participants to return the twelve o'clock toothpick to its original twelve o'clock position before proceeding with Item 2 in Figure 5-2. Ask them to complete that figure now.

Two cautionary comments: (1) At this point, participants are to vary only *one* line at a time. This procedure is appropriate here even though in reality more than one line will move at a time as new events occur. The limitation is appropriate, however, in order to become involved with The Supervision Window, which goes from simplicity to complexity. (2) Participants may have a difficult time thinking of a possible cause for each of the eight variations. No matter. This will offer an excellent point to discuss later in the debriefing. The point here is mainly to get acquainted with the varying panes by actually seeing some of the essential movements.

Use Figure 5-7 in guiding the participants through the eight variations of moving the toothpicks. Do not indicate to the participants the contents of Figure 5-7 as they proceed, because the object is for them to use their own ideas. You will later discuss their responses as you debrief this activity.

Step 6.   When the participants have completed Figure 5-2, ask them to return the toothpicks to their initial positions. Now ask them, in light of their familiarity with The Supervision Window, its variations and their possible causes, to make up three more possible windows. "Suppose that it is September, the beginning of a new school year. You

1	twelve o'clock	Right	Public	Blind	Observation by supervisor and reported to teacher in conference afterwards

FIGURE 5-6. First row of worksheet indicating change of twelve o'clock line of The Supervision Window.

	1	2	3	4	5
	Line	Move In Direction*	Area That Expands	Area That Shrinks	Cause
1	12 o'clock	Right	Public	Blind	observations by supervisor reported to teacher in conference afterwards
2	9 o'clock	Up	Private	Public	teacher self-help on deficiencies; lack of ongoing observations
3	9 o'clock	Down	Public	Private	teacher confiding with supervisor as teacher grows and develops
4	6 o'clock	Right	Private	Unperceived	self-help and introspection about new dimensions of teaching; lack of T-S talk
5	12 o'clock	Left	Blind	Public	supervisor observes but no feedback to T; lack of self-examination by T
6	3 o'clock	Down	Blind	Unperceived	observation without feedback
7	3 o'clock	Up	Unperceived	Blind	lack of observation of T; routinized and unsupervised T is not introspective
8	6 o'clock	Left	Unperceived	Private	routine teaching without observation; T not self-aware

*Before moving the next line, be sure to replace the previous line in its original position.

FIGURE 5-7. Completed worksheet for The Supervision Window.

have a new addition to your faculty whom you met two weeks ago. She is not a beginning teacher. You are to begin supervising this teacher. What will this teacher's Supervision Window look like as you begin supervision with her in September? What do you expect it to look like in mid-January? What do you expect it to look like by June? Move the toothpicks *in any direction and in any angle* to indicate the expansion and shrinking of the four quadrants. Move as many toothpicks as you want in order to arrive at the right size of the window panes as you see them. After you form each of the three windows—

"September," "January," "June"—sketch and label the window in pencil on a piece of paper for later reference. Keep in mind that because it is impossible to eliminate any area 100 percent, the numbers of the quadrants appear in the corners and guide you always to leave at least this much of the quadrants present." Distribute a piece of paper to each person for sketching the three figures, or see the alternative approach under Item 3 in "Suggestions and Comments." (For your use, three possible responses appear in Figure 5-8.)

Step 7. Distribute a copy of Figure 5-9 and four more toothpicks to each participant. At this point, you introduce the recognition, if it has not yet arisen, that the supervisor has his or her own window just as the teacher does. The supervisor, in relation to the teacher, has Public, Blind, Private, and Unperceived areas. This is shown in Figure 5-9, where the supervisor's window is on the left in a flip position in order to show the Public areas of the teacher and supervisor facing each other. For example, the supervisor's Public quadrant refers to what the teacher and supervisor know in common *about the supervisor*. The teacher's and supervisor's Public areas need not be the same size as they may share more things about the teacher than about the supervisor.

This recognition is important when you realize that in a conference the supervisor will be revealing things he or she knows not only about the teacher but about him- or herself. The interaction between supervisor and teacher, however, is focused on the teacher's window in order to shrink the Blind, Private, and Unperceived areas and to expand the Public area so as to lead to teacher development. *Nevertheless, though the primary purpose of supervision is obviously not the growth of the supervisor, the supervisor's perspective (as shown by his window) is influenced by the teacher at the same time the supervisor is influencing the teacher.* Therefore, the changes appearing in the teacher's window, especially those stemming from conferring, will be influencing the supervisor's window and vice versa. That is to say, though supervision focuses on changing the teacher's awareness (as shown by his Supervision Window), the supervisor's awareness (as shown by his window) is of significance because of the important interactive effect it has.

FIGURE 5-8. Possible supervision windows of a teacher during a school year.

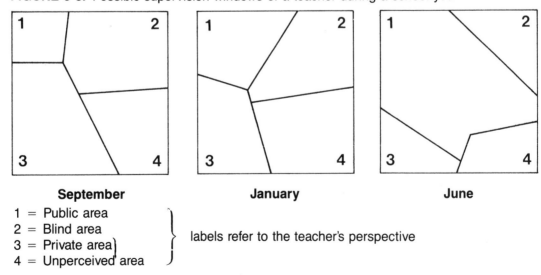

September   January   June

1 = Public area
2 = Blind area
3 = Private area } labels refer to the teacher's perspective
4 = Unperceived area

Concerning Supervisor

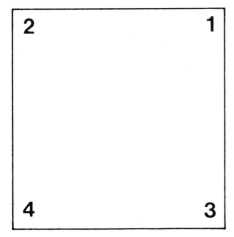

Concerning Teacher

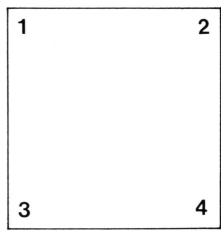

1 = Public area   2 = Blind area   3 = Private area   4 = Unperceived area

FIGURE 5-9. Supervision windows of teacher and supervisor.

It is in this light that you should ask the participants to use their toothpicks to form two beginning windows with four equal quadrants each. Then, on Figure 5-9 ask them to form on the right side their September window for the teachers. In light of this change, they should now indicate on the left side any changes in the supervisor's window. This sequence of moving the lines is not intended to imply that the teacher's changes cause the supervisor's changes. Rather, there is an interactive change with each window's changes causing the other's to change. Each is both cause and effect. Then ask the participants to form the two January windows; ask them to form the two June windows. In each of these three interactions ask the participants to start with the teacher's window but to go back and forth between it and the supervisor's window, adjusting each in light of the other, until they arrive at September, January, and June pairs of windows. This shows the interaction of awareness between teacher and supervisor. Distribute a piece of paper to each person for sketching the three pairs of figures, or see the alternative approach under Item 4 in "Suggestions and Comments." (For *your guidance* three possible responses appear in Figures 5-10, 5-11, and 5-12 based on the responses already presented in Figure 5-8.)

Step 8. Debrief. As you debrief, try to keep your role as discussion facilitator and paraphraser. Try not to "preach" to the group. Patience will pay off.

Read "Points Raised by Activity" to alert yourself to the points that generally come out during the debriefing section. Do not try to force more points than the group is willing to initiate because the forced points probably will not be meaningful anyway. Keep the extra points in mind, note them, and raise them at another time to your faculty when you wish to relate evaluation to the teaching process and to supervision.

Note that there are many sample questions below. You will no doubt not need to ask every question since many of the points will come to the floor without solicitation. Ask only those questions you want to ask and need to ask in order to keep the discussion going.

Concerning Supervisor

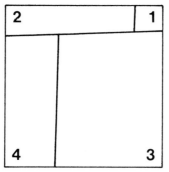

Concerning Teacher

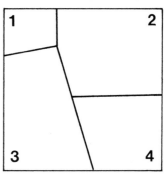

1 = Public area
2 = Blind area
3 = Private area
4 = Unperceived area

FIGURE 5-10. Supervision windows of teacher and supervisor in September.

Concerning Supervisor

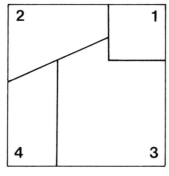

Concerning Teacher

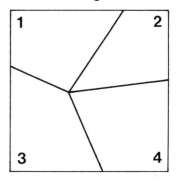

1 = Public area
2 = Blind area
3 = Private area
4 = Unperceived area

FIGURE 5-11. Supervision windows of teacher and supervisor in January.

Follow the debriefing strategy below so you can reap the benefits of this structured activity.

1. Shift into the debriefing session by simply and only saying something like, "Now let's talk about what happened."
2. Begin the discussion by encouraging the *participants to describe what happened*. Let them "ventilate" and "show and tell" about their windows. Without sufficient hard-fact ventilation and showing there will not be an adequate basis for making discoveries and drawing conclusions later on. This opening phase of the debriefing will loosen up the group and get them talking, as it is very easy to talk on this concrete, nonthreatening level. Ask such questions as: In Figure 5-2 what are your responses for Row 1? Row 2? Row 3? Row 4? Row 5? Row 6? Row 7? Row 8? Were any rows easier to

Concerning Supervisor

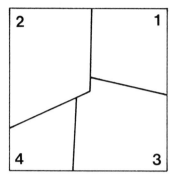

Concerning Teacher

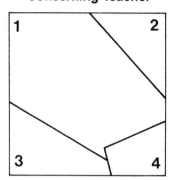

1 = Public area
2 = Blind area
3 = Private area
4 = Unperceived area

FIGURE 5-12. Supervision windows of teacher and supervisor in June.

work with than the others? Are there any causes which appear more than once? What does your September window look like for the teacher? Your January window? Your June window? From Figure 5-9 what does your September pair of windows look like? Your January pair of windows? Your June pair of windows? On what basis or bases did you form the supervisor's window in each of the three cases? What difficulty, if any, did you have forming the supervisor's window in light of the teacher's window?

3. *Analyze the data, including the causes and the newly formed windows, and the points of this structured activity.* Discuss what the "toothpick ballet" adds up to; discuss the meaning of the causes of the changes in The Supervision Window of Figure 5-3 and Figure 5-9. Ask such questions as: Which of the causes can you easily bring about? How can you help a teacher shrink his Blind area in a way that doesn't lead to defensiveness? How can you establish trust so that the teacher is willing and ready to expand the Public area at the expense of his private area? How can you ethically work on shrinking the Unperceived area when neither of you—teacher or supervisor—knows the specifics? (For example, is it ethical to speak to students about the teacher's behavior? If so, to what degree can you probe students and still not be unethical or hurt the teacher?) What steps can you take to lead the September window to change into January and the January window to change into June? How does the window of the supervisor affect the teacher's window? In addition to *awareness* of what is known and unknown, what concepts does The Supervision Window activity present to us? What is the optimum size of each of the four areas of a teacher's window after a year of solid supervision?

4. *Examine the implications of this activity for teaching and supervision.* Ask such questions as: With a beginning teacher, how should you go about expanding the "public" area in the most supportive way? Are there any rules or guidelines for the supervisor to follow based on the ideas talked about in this activity? What implications are there for teaching based on this activity? Implications for observing? Implications for conferring? In what ways can we modify The Supervision Window so it will have meaning for teachers and students interacting in the classroom?

5. *Summarize, generalize, conclude.* Tie the many points together by asking for a general message conveyed by the activity. Do not assume that the participants will

generalize and draw conclusions on their own without guidance. Ask such questions as: From all that we have said and done, what conclusions do you draw from this activity? What overall generalization can you offer about the role of awareness in supervision?

If you wish, you can do the summarizing in a different way. You can request the participants to list some key ideas that have come forth during the debriefing discussion and to offer some generalizations based on these key ideas. This approach is effective since the generalizations grow immediately and directly from what the group says. You can initiate this approach by asking each person to complete whichever of the following sentence stems you feel is more appropriate:

Based on this activity, I realize about my interaction in teaching that

_____

Based on this activity, I realize about my interaction in supervision that

_____

Be sure to ask the group to read their completed sentences.

Step 9.   Move forward. Before leaving The Supervision Window behind, structure the activity so that you launch yourself and the group into something new built on it. In this way, you bridge current activity with future activity while interest is high. You can build, perhaps, on one of the ideas raised in the summary part of your debriefing, especially if you have utilized the alternative summary approach, which specifically elicits what people have realized from the activity. See the "Applications" section later in this chapter for further ideas.

POINTS RAISED BY ACTIVITY

   1.   *Awareness of feelings, beliefs, skills, behaviors, and ideas is fundamental to teacher development and sound supervision.* The first step in changing is awareness. Once the teacher is aware of what is happening—aware of his behaviors, in particular— the teacher can proceed to implement new ideas and skills that will lead to change in his classroom. However, it may take a while to move from X to Y because of habit and because of some natural resistance. Change may come slowly, but the first step is awareness of what is known and unknown and awareness of how people interact in relation to what is known and unknown.

   2.   *The more open a teacher and supervisor are between them the easier it is to establish a developmental relationship that can lead to professional growth.* If the teacher and you as supervisor begin to trust each other based on a record of behavior that promotes further trust, then the teacher and you can begin to interact in a way that expands the teacher's Public area of his Supervision Window. With trust as the cornerstone, you can observe and confer with the teacher with the good intent of helping the teacher shrink the Blind, Private, and Unperceived areas of his teaching life. The result will be the expansion of the Public area, which is the foundation of a relationship leading to growth. A teacher who interacts in an open, public way is able to receive feedback about his teaching, which can lead to further growth.

The open relationship between teacher and supervisor, though focused on the teacher's behavior and beliefs, requires that you the supervisor be open yourself. As mentioned earlier, it is clear and accepted that the purpose of supervision is the development of the teacher. Nevertheless, the supervisor's own sense of awareness and openness, as shown by the Public, Private, Blind, and Unperceived areas of his Supervision Window, influences the teacher. If you maintain large Blind and Private areas and restrain yourself from sharing beliefs, knowledge, and skills with the teacher, then the interaction between the two of you is not smooth and facilitative of growth. If the teacher is the only person to change and grow, the relationship is not as helpful as it might be. For optimal development both the teacher and you need to be open to each other. The more open the teacher and you are to each other—larger Public areas in the Supervision Window—the greater the potential for professional growth for both of you.

3. *A change in one area of the teacher's behavior affects other areas as well.* If the teacher and you, through classroom observations and conferences, succeed in reducing the teacher's Blind quadrant, it is very likely that both the teacher's Private and Unperceived areas will change along with the Public area. The teacher, like every human being, is a whole, undivided person. Although you may use the four quadrants of The Supervision Window to aid yourself in understanding the teacher's awareness of his actions, the teacher is but one person. Therefore, any single aspect of his life overlaps onto several other areas. If the teacher becomes better known to you as supervisor, for example, by shrinking his Private area, then other changes will result. For example, because the Public area expands, you will interact differently and more openly with the teacher, leading the teacher to trust you more. This, in turn, may lead to more confiding by the teacher (reducing the Private quadrant). In short, change leads to further change in the other aspects of the teacher's life.

Figure 5-13 shows some of the multiple changes in the interaction between a teacher and you as supervisor. The prime communication between the two of you is from Public area to Public area (Lines A and B). These two areas are shared knowledge about

FIGURE 5-13. Supervision windows of teacher and supervisor showing levels of communication during a post-observation conference.

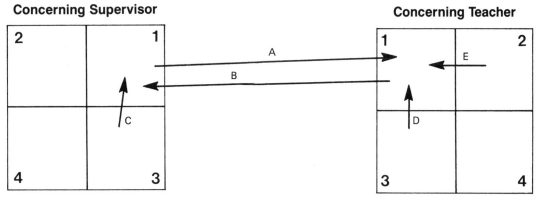

Concerning Supervisor

Concerning Teacher

1 = Public area
2 = Blind area
3 = Private area
4 = Unperceived area

each other. As a post-observation conference progresses, part of the teacher's Blind area shifts into the Public area (Line E) due to your report. Meanwhile, you are offering values, goals, and expectations that are part of your Private area. This knowledge then shifts into your Public area (Line C). These changes during the conferences may well elicit some further change in the teacher's window as shown by Line D. Here, the teacher begins to talk about his experiences so far unknown to you. This shift occurs through the communication by moving some Private material into the teacher's Public quadrant. These shifts are simultaneous and often go unnoticed, resulting in a constantly changing Supervision Window for each of you that then has a different effect on the other person.

4. *A supervisor must be aware of and sensitive to the teacher's Blind and Private areas.* As supervisor you must recognize that communication takes place on several levels simultaneously. As you are conferring about what was observed in the classroom during an observation visit, you are reporting data that will shrink the teacher's Blind area. You must be sensitive to the realization that the teacher may find it painful to learn about an area he or she does not know about. Indeed, the teacher may have expended much energy in protecting his Blind area in order to keep it from shrinking, feeling safer about not knowing than knowing, believing that what he doesn't know won't hurt him, and realizing that knowing inevitably will bring about change that will cause some further pain.

During the same conference, the teacher may be confiding in you as supervisor and thus enlarging the Public area at the expense of the Private area. You must recognize that this act of confiding conveys three messages simultaneously: (1) The teacher trusts you and feels comfortable enough to reveal personal feelings, beliefs, and knowledge about which you don't know. This is a complimentary message. (2) The teacher may be feeling awkward or pained or guilty as he reveals things to you. This act of revealing may be a struggle for the teacher at the same time that he feels good about the relationship with you as supervisor. (3) The teacher is willing and ready to take a needed step toward further development—the expansion of his Public area. This sharing with you is a needed step toward further growth because as the Public area expands, trust develops even more and this in turn leads to even greater potential for growth. You need to respond in a way which recognizes the messages and say verbally and/or nonverbally, "Thanks for confiding; I recognize that you're struggling; let's try to build on that."

In short, as you confer with a teacher you must recognize that communication and change are occurring on several levels simultaneously. Furthermore, the teacher is sending several messages at the same time regarding his Supervision Window, and these messages have influence on your own behavior vis-a-vis the teacher. Though you are rightfully concerned with the teacher's Public area because you have shared knowledge there, you must be sensitive to the other areas as well.

5. *It is not possible nor desirable to eliminate the Blind, Private, and Unperceived areas of the teacher as you seek to expand the Public area.* As the teacher continues to teach while supervision is ongoing, the teacher's Blind and Private areas continue to grow. New things are occurring each day in the classroom, and no supervisor—which includes you—can ever know all that the teacher is doing, feeling, and believing. Moreover, each individual needs to have some privacy. It is too painful and it is unhealthy to be exposed totally to other people or even one other person. It is normal for self-protection and maintenance of self that the teacher keep certain things Private and even be Blind to other things. For this reason, it is unwise for you as supervisor to try to eliminate the Blind, Private, and Unperceived areas and to make the teacher's Supervision Window 100 percent Public.

6. *People communicate messges from their Blind area, though they may forget and deny it, to which other people react.* The teacher, as noted above, is sending several messages simultaneously to you during your observations and conferences. You pick up the message because you are open to it. Even though you may not have empirical data to confirm the feelings you have about the teacher, you may be reacting to the messages you have received. You may believe that the knowledge is now Public, and you may then speak openly about the teacher in a way which reflects the message. However, since the message is from the teacher's Blind area, the teacher may not understand what you are saying. For the teacher there is no shared knowledge. This miscommunication or poor communication arises because the source of the message is the Blind area, and you may treat it as Public.

7. *A teacher's value system dictates the preference he has about the relative size of each of the four areas of his Supervision Window.* Because different people vary in regard to the value they set on awareness, openness, and privacy, the willingness a teacher has to explore his Blind, Private, and Unperceived areas with you will be an individual matter. Some people, either because of their upbringing at home or their community's cultural values, put great emphasis on individual privacy not only in the political sphere but also the professional sphere. Notwithstanding the recognition that professional growth results from openness to help and counsel from other professionals, a given teacher may value privacy so highly as to feel uncomfortable with you as you seek to emphasize openness—the enlargement of the Public area partially at the expense of the Private area.

As supervisor, you must seek to differentiate between (1) the teacher who seeks to keep his Private area large out of fear that your knowledge of his affairs will lead to your power over him and (2) the teacher who seeks to keep his Private area large because of a fundamental value prizing the individuality of each person. The former acts out of fear that you will gain power to control him; the latter acts out of belief that a strong individual is someone who is independent and can deal with matters on his own. The implications for your subsequent behavior are different for each. With the former, you will need to take steps to demonstrate that you are not engaged in a win/lose power play with the teacher. With the latter, you need to talk openly about values and avenues leading to development of the individual teacher within the social school.

8. *The teacher's Unperceived area is a significant source of potential growth.* The Unperceived area is the area of mystery since neither the teacher or you knows what is there. As with other areas of mystery in our lives, a frontal attack to expose the Unperceived area is no doubt a strategic error. Nevertheless, as long as you recognize its existence, you can come eventually to understand some of the behaviors and feelings of the teacher. You need to be ethical and restrained in dealing with this Unperceived area. As you concern yourself mainly with the other three areas, the Unperceived area will begin to shrink, and your task is then to be alert enough to deal with perceptions arising from the Unperceived area.

9. *The communication of feelings between teacher and supervisor is often the Blind area of one person sending messages to the Blind area of the other.* Many, if not most, people do not verbalize their emotions. This is accepted in our society. Nevertheless, the feelings are present and other people may recognize them and understand them without hearing an explicit announcement or explanation of them. Though the teacher may not realize that he is disappointed, you may know how he feels and rightly react to his disappointment. You may try to implement activities that will change his perspective. However, if you are not sensitive to his feelings, you may be affected and not know it. You, in turn will be sending messages to the teacher unaware of the process yourself. On the other hand, the initiative may be yours. That is, from your Blind area may come a message of satisfaction and approval that the teacher receives and integrates unknown to him. In either case, there are emotions that may be caught by the other person unconsciously, much like a person catches a cold and then gives it to someone else without even realizing it.

SUGGESTIONS AND COMMENTS

1. You can use this Supervision Window activity with teachers or supervisors. Because the activity deals with perspectives on awareness and openness, probably it will be better to have both teachers and supervisors present so that participants can speak about the two perspectives from their own personal vantage points. But no matter who is among your participants it will be helpful for you to read the "Points Raised by Activity" in order to decide the direction you will take regarding emphasis—teacher's perspective, supervisor's perspective, or both perspectives in balance.

2. In general, in structured activities the debriefing occurs *after* the "doing" phase of the activity. However, in this Supervision Window activity you might find it helpful and natural to do a mini-debriefing after Step 5 and Step 6 of the conducting strategy. If you do so, you then will launch your regular debriefing after Step 7 with another mini-debriefing regarding Step 7 before discussing the overall issues for this activity. Keep in mind that if you conduct mini-debriefings after Steps 5, 6, and 7, you should limit yourself in time and scope. You must do this lest you get so involved in talking that you don't move on to other parts of the strategy. A mini-debriefing is in keeping with the belief some people hold that a debriefing is too important to leave to the end of the allotted time. Do what is comfortable and better for you and don't lose sight of the overall picture and strategy.

3. In Step 6 of the "Procedure" the direction calls for distributing a piece of blank paper on which the participants are to sketch the windows they form for September, January, and June. An alternative to this approach is to distribute two additional copies of Figure 5-3 to each person. Participants can then use their three copies of the figure to work on, sketch, and label the three windows for September, January, and June. You could even distribute extra toothpicks with the three copies of the figure so that all three figures are variable before sketching and labeling them.

4. Similar to the alternative above, in Step 7 of the strategy you could distribute extra copies of Figure 5-9 along with extra toothpicks. In this way participants could work out each pair of windows for September, January, and June before sketching and labeling them.

5. If you are *very* pressed for time, you may be able to combine Steps 6 and 7 of the conducting strategy. You may save some time, but you will need to be careful about introducing the two ideas of *changeover time* and *interacting windows* simultaneously. Two ideas together may prove too much to handle as you give directions. Take extra care to explain your procedures if you do decide to combine these steps.

6. You can conduct this activity in about seventy-five minutes. If you have more time, you can go slowly in Steps 5, 6, and 7 as the participants work with the toothpicks. Participants enjoy moving the toothpicks around to form various windows, especially when the windows are interactive. Whatever you decide, leave at least thirty minutes for debriefing in Step 8 and moving forward in Step 9. These two steps are most important since they allow you to relate the windows formed to your particular supervisory situation.

7. If you are department head, for example, and do not feel comfortable leading this activity with your faculty, by all means ask someone else to lead it. Perhaps the school principal or a district supervisor will lead this activity for you. You can be a participant or observer, as you see fit.

APPLICATIONS

The Supervision Window goes to the heart of the supervisory process. The theme of the activity—awareness and openness—pertains to every teacher and supervisor. When people stop being aware of what is occurring around them and with them, they lapse into routinized behavior, a deadly condition for effectiveness. When professionals cease to be open to interactive communication, which aims to arouse awareness, the potential for further development is low. For these reasons all educators must remain aware of what they are doing and what other people are communicating to them. All educators need to "see" clearly the impact of their known and unknown areas vis-à-vis the people to whom they are responsible.

As with all structured activities, the ideas talked about by the participants need to be followed up. Specific steps, even if they appear to be unimportant ones at the time, need to be taken so that change can take place along preferred lines. What appears unimportant may indeed be unimportant by itself, but it may be the activating means to other, more important steps.

SPECIAL MEMO

In Figure 5-14 it is clear that one group decided to concentrate on their Blind areas once they realized the potential for growth that lay in what they didn't know about themselves. The unknown or partially unknown areas of our lives are a source of tremendous growth. Yet it takes courage to be willing to seek the unknown and tap it as a resource. To minimize the danger or threat from exposing their Blind spots, the group of teachers used peer observations rather than supervisor observations. They felt that they could talk with colleagues more easily and effectively as they faced what they might have refused to face previously. This no doubt goes along with the third key point mentioned, referring to respect for the unknown as important in education. (An example of a completed memo is shown in Figure 5-15.)

TO: _____

FROM: _____

RE: Follow-up from The Supervision Window

   Led by _____ on _____, 19___

1. Quotable quotes from the session:

   A.

   B.

   C.

2. Key points raised:

   A.

   B.

   C.

3. Decisions to follow through for implementation:

FIGURE 5-14. Follow-up memo for The Supervision Window (blank).

TO: Faculty, Science and Math Departments

FROM: Grace Talper

RE: Follow-up from The Supervision Window

   Led by Gerry   on Aug. 30 , 19XX

1. Quotable quotes from the session:

   A. Awareness begets change begets awareness.

   B. I "see" through my "window" much more clearly now.

   C. Yes, it is true that in our society the Public must pay attention to the Blind.

2. Key points raised:

   A. Parts of us talk to other people in different ways all the time.

   B. Awareness and openness are fundamentals to our professional progress.

   C. Respect for the unknown is a prerequisite for its discovery.

3. Decisions to follow through for implementation:
   Each person agreed to prepare a short list of items for visitors to observe to help us all become more aware of our blind spots. Please post your list on the faculty bulletin board by Sept. 5 so we can begin our peer visitations prepared.

FIGURE 5-15. Follow-up memo for The Supervision Window (filled in).

SUPERVISION

When you meet with your faculty during the year, you can periodically pull out Figure 5-3 or Figure 5-9 and some toothpicks to ask for an on-the-spot assessment by the teachers of their own current situations and yours. You can use the windows formed as a springboard for a conference and planning session for what you should observe and confer about in your forthcoming classroom visit. You can use the window as a bridging scheme to motivate and organize teachers, whereby the window metaphor helps you to see the teacher's perspective, and the concepts of Public, Private, Blind, and Unperceived areas can promote fruitful bridging.

By referring to the chapters on observing in the companion book, *Administrator's Faculty Supervision Handbook*, you and your teachers can select the techniques that will provide you with the most suitable ways to bring about awareness and openness in your teachers, your fellow supervisors, and yourself. The techniques presented in that book dovetail with the ideas of this structured activity. They support the Public areas and expand them by drawing from the Blind and Private areas of teachers and supervisors alike. You can arrange for observation by peers or you, as supervisor, can observe.

CONCLUDING WORDS

The Supervision Window offers a fruitful way to view the interaction you have with teachers. It offers a view which emphasizes two concepts fundamental to growth—awareness and openness. It recognizes that people differ in what they know about themselves and what others know about them. It accepts that people have Private selves and Blind spots. It allows you to see the several dimensions of your teacher while seeing the whole teacher.

The Supervision Window activity offers the opportunity to become acquainted with the theme of awareness and openness by varying the internal dimensions of The Supervision Window's structure. It promotes an understanding of the interactive effects between the teacher and you as supervisor. Because the faculty and you can manipulate the panes of the window concretely, you can come to understand its meaning in a meaningful way. You can see change in its stages and change in one person affecting another person. The activity, because it is simple in design, promotes an open and pleasant way to discuss awareness, which is the beginning of growth.

CHAPTER 5 ENDNOTE

1. JOSEPH LUFT, *Of Human Interaction* (Palo Alto, CA: National Press Books, 1969).

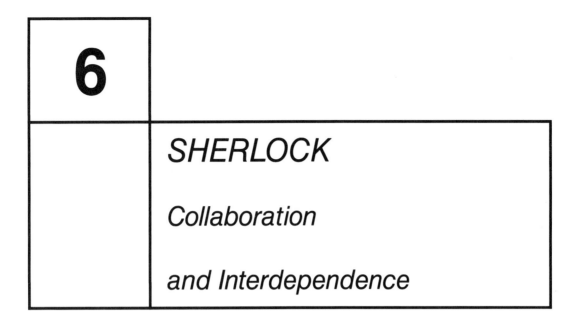

SHERLOCK

Collaboration

and Interdependence

In Sherlock, named after the most well-known fictional detective, participants solve a mystery based on some clues given to them. As a structured activity, Sherlock involves participants in deductive thinking as they sift through clues to solve the mystery. Participants succeed only because they work together in a particular way, demonstrating the power of collaborative interdependence. In a short time, participants can feel what happens when the rules governing their actions require interdependence. Although the theme is familiar, it is, nevertheless, striking and applicable to supervision and to teaching.

After reading this chapter, you should be able to:

- Understand the purpose of, steps for, and points raised by Sherlock.
- Conduct Sherlock confidently with your faculty following the step-by-step strategy.
- Describe at least five points raised that relate to collaborative interdependence.
- List at least two ways you can apply the points raised in the debriefing discussion to your supervision of the faculty.

OVERVIEW

In Sherlock participants form small "whodunit groups" of four to seven people. Each person receives several clues to a mystery which the group is to solve together. The leader announces some Baker Street rules to abide by as the group seeks to put its clues together to form a solution. After each group succeeds in solving the mystery, all the participants discuss what happened in their groups, their methods of procedure, and the points raised by this activity.

MATERIALS NEEDED

Two scenarios with clues are given here so that you may choose one. Sherlock Plant[1] (see Figures 6-1 and 6-2) deals with solving the mystery of Elizabeth Smith's favorite house plant. Sherlock Dinosaur[2] (see Figures 6-3 and 6-4) deals with solving the mystery of a bone found in an excavation in Montana. Both Sherlock whodunits work well. It is a matter of your choice as to which one to use with your faculty. Sherlock Plant is a bit easier to use as it does not contain many technical and unfamiliar words. For this reason, it is placed first and referred to in the chapter.

Whichever you choose, you will need a scenario for each person and a set of whodunit clues for *each* group of four to seven people. Cut the clues into strips, one clue per strip, and place the complete set into an unsealed envelope.

NUMBER OF PARTICIPANTS

There is no limit to the number of people who can participate in this activity at the same time. The minimum is four. Organize participants into small groups of four to seven people, *preferably five or six to a group*. With some juggling of group size you can accommodate a large number of people. You can also:

1. Assign at least one person from the total group to take the role of observer/enforcer. The observer/enforcer takes mental and written notes of what happens during Sherlock; the observer/enforcer helps you enforce the whodunit rules which you will announce to the group. For a large group you might want to use more than one observer/enforcer.

2. Create jacks-in-the-box, that is, two people who work alternately as one participant. One stands behind the other. At a cue from you—after a few minutes—the jacks switch positions. The jack who was sitting pops up to take the place of the jack who was standing and vice versa. The former standing jack now works with the other participants in the group to solve the mystery. *The two jacks may talk to each other only when switching positions.*

PROCEDURE

Step 1. Introduce this activity *very briefly*. Simply ask the group to join you in an activity which you believe is beneficial to all of you as will be evident in the ensuing discussion. Be sure not to reveal what will happen. The idea is for the group to realize on its own what has happened when they debrief in Step 9. So, say little and be brief in order to get the activity going quickly. The scenario to be distributed soon will help you.

Step 2. Organize the participants into small groups of four to seven participants, preferably five or six in a group. Assign someone to be observer/enforcer and some people to be jacks-in-the-box, if desired and needed. (See "Number of Participants" for details and comments on grouping the participants.)

Elizabeth Smith is 85 years old and retired from the county agricultural department. She raises plants as a hobby. She reads avidly about plants and has over 100 plants in her greenhouse. She keeps other plants in window locations in her house. Since her windows face east, south, west, and north, she uses the locations to control the amount of sun the plants get.

Elizabeth Smith recently broke her hip when she tripped and fell while walking to the mailbox to order some seeds by mail. Right now she is in the hospital. It is mid-December. You want to surprise her by bringing her favorite kind of plant to her, but you don't know which one it is.

You are Sherlock Plant, a well known plant expert and detective. Through your knowledge and insight as a detective you have collected a set of clues about Elizabeth Smith's plants. To help you sift this evidence, you have set up five questions which will identify Elizabeth Smith's favorite plant and help you instruct the hospital staff as to its care. Here are the questions:

1. What kind of flower pot is the plant in—clay pot? plastic pot? glazed dish-type pot? hanging pot?

2. What kind of plant is it—begonia? azalea? philodendron? asparagus fern? Christmas cactus? spider plant?

3. Is the plant now near the east, west, north, or south window?

4. How much water should you give the plant—water it a medium amount? water it well? water it very well? water it exceedingly well?

5. Is it in bloom? If so, are the flowers white or pink?

If you answer all five questions correctly, you will solve the mystery and know which is Elizabeth Smith's favorite plant.

FIGURE 6-1. Scenario for Sherlock Plant.

1. Elizabeth Smith told you that it would be good to see some of her plants from the east window.
2. You know that Elizabeth Smith is especially fond of flowering plants, so you will bring a plant that is in bloom.
3. The Christmas cactus's rosy pink or red flowers bloom at year's end.
4. Philodendrons do not have flowers.
5. Asparagus ferns need a lot of water. Water them very well.
6. Asparagus ferns do not like full sunlight. Therefore, no asparagus ferns are in Elizabeth Smith's south window.
7. Elizabeth Smith's philodendrons are in her east and north windows.
8. The azalea must not be allowed to dry out. In the growing season, water them exceedingly well and mist frequently.
9. All Elizabeth Smith's azaleas are in clay pots.
10. None of Elizabeth Smith's flowering azaleas is white.
11. Early in December Elizabeth Smith moved her budding azalea plants to the east and west windows to keep them in bloom longer.
12. Elizabeth Smith put some begonias in glazed dish-type pots.
13. Most of the begonias are in the west window. The rest are in the south window.
14. Elizabeth Smith's wax begonias have white flowers.
15. Elizabeth Smith's philodendrons and begonias need a medium amount of water in December.
16. Only two plants that flower are in Elizabeth Smith's east window.
17. The south window in Elizabeth Smith's house gets lots of direct sunlight, about five hours a day.
18. Elizabeth Smith's begonias and azaleas are in bloom.
19. None of Elizabeth Smith's Christmas cacti, asparagus ferns, or spider plants are in bloom.
20. All Elizabeth Smith's flowering plants that do not have white flowers have pink ones.
21. Philodendrons need bright light but little sun.
22. Elizabeth Smith put some philodendrons in plastic pots.
23. In December, all Elizabeth Smith's Christmas cacti are in the south window where they get full sun.
24. Wax begonias flower freely from October to June.
25. Elizabeth Smith's east and west windows get direct sunlight for about two hours each day. Plants that need small amounts of sun do well in the east and west windows.
26. The spider plant produces white flowers on its flower stalks.
27. The spider plant has a grass-like appearance. It grows easily when kept well watered and well fed.
28. From late fall to early spring, Elizabeth Smith waters her Christmas cacti well. She reduces the amount of water once the plants stop blooming.
29. In December Elizabeth Smith's azaleas require more water than her asparagus ferns.
30. Elizabeth Smith has begonias, azaleas, and asparagus ferns in clay pots.

FIGURE 6-2. Clues for Sherlock Plant.

While excavating for a new highway through sedimentary rock in southeastern Montana, a bulldozer operator unearthed what looked like a bone. He stopped his machine to examine the object and showed it to his boss, who notified a friend at the local museum. Since the object looked like a big bone, the experts at the Museum of Natural History came to study the site. The highway excavation was temporarily halted.

Museum paleontologists chipped away the chalk deposits around the object slowly. They finally released a lower jawbone with sharp-edged teeth at the front end. The bone was straight from hinge to front and it measured 4 feet long.

You are Sherlock Dinosaur, well-known dinosaur expert, author, and consultant to the museum. The museum has hired you to study the evidence and identify the nature of the object. Using the clues given, you must sift the evidence to answer the following questions:

1. What order of dinosaur was this—Ornithischia or Saurischia?

2. What kind of dinosaur was it—*Triceratops, Allosaurus*, or *Tyrannosaurus Rex*?

3. When did it live—185 million years ago, 150 million years ago, or 100 million years ago?

4. Was it herbivorous or carnivorous?

5. Did it walk on two feet or four?

If you answer all five questions correctly, you will solve the mystery and know which dinosaur is the source of the jawbone.

FIGURE 6-3. Scenario for Sherlock Dinosaur.

1. The two-footed ancestors of all dinosaurs from the Triassic period gave rise to two main orders of dinosaurs, Ornithischia and Saurischia.
2. In Ornithischian dinosaurs, teeth were found only on the sides of the jaw.
3. In geology, time is divided into five major sections called eras. Each era is then subdivided into periods, and each period is subdivided into epochs.
4. *Allosaurus* had a jaw 2½ feet long and measured 30 feet from nose to tail.
5. On the sides of its beaked jaw, *Triceratops*, last of the great horned dinosaurs, had sharp, shearing teeth that meshed like scissors blades to slice fibrous and woody plants.
6. Saurischian dinosaurs gave rise to two main suborders of dinosaurs: Theropods and Sauropods.
7. Theropods walked on two hind legs and used small front legs for grasping and tearing food.
8. *Allosaurus* flourished during the Jurassic period.
9. Chalk is the most characteristic deposit of the Cretaceous period.
10. *Tyrannosaurus Rex* was able to bite 100-pound chunks of meat at a time.
11. *Tyrannosaurus Rex* was longer than *Allosaurus*, its ancestor, by about 20 feet.
12. *Tyrannosaurus Rex* was a Theropod with front legs so very small they weren't long enough to reach its large mouth. The two hind legs of this animal were very powerful.
13. The Mesozoic Era had three time periods: Cretaceous (60–130 million years ago); Jurassic (130–170 million years ago); and Triassic (170–200 million years ago).
14. Saurischia is pronounced *saw Riss ki uh*.
15. Ornithischia is pronounced *or ni THIS ki uh*.
16. Dinosaurs are a type of reptile.
17. The word "dinosaur" comes from the Greek "dinos" (terrible) and "sauros" (lizard). Though dinosaurs were not lizards, the big flesh-eating ones were terrible.
18. *Triceratops*, like the modern rhinoceros, defended itself against attackers like *Tyrannosaurus Rex* by charging at them. In this way *Triceratops* used its horns as a counterattack weapon.
19. Theropods preyed on plant-eating dinosaurs and were mainly carnivorous.
20. Theropods had big heads and used their large sharp front teeth for biting their food.
21. Sauropods were gigantic plant-eating dinosaurs with delicate teeth; they had long necks and tails and must have eaten only tender plants.
22. Dinosaurs appeared in the late Triassic period and died out at the end of the Cretaceous period.
23. Sauropods were herbivorous and generally walked on four feet.
24. During the Cretaceous period a suborder named Ceratops developed from the order Ornithischia. Ceratops dinosaurs were herbivorous, four-footed dinosaurs with horns on their heads.
25. Sedimentary rock is formed by layers of materials being deposited on top of each other and buried for millions of years.
26. The Rocky Mountain area of Montana was the home of many dinosaurs during the Mesozoic Era. At that time, however, it was neither rocky nor mountainous. The terrain was flat and had many swamps, rivers, and lakes.
27. Saurischian dinosaurs and Ornithischian dinosaurs differed in the structure of the pelvis, or hip bone. Saurischians had hips similar to those of modern lizards; Ornithischians had bird-like hips.
28. Scientists learn about dinosaurs from fossils.
29. *Triceratops* means "three horned," and the *Triceratops* is one type of Ceratops dinosaur.
30. Red sandstone is typical of Triassic deposits.

FIGURE 6-4. Clues for Sherlock Dinosaur.

Step 3.   Distribute a copy of the scenario to each person and ask everyone to read it carefully. Review the five questions with the group to be sure the scenario and whodunit task are clear; make sure the mystery is clear.

Step 4.   Distribute an envelope of clues to someone in each group. Ask the distributor for each group to distribute carefully all the strips randomly among the participants as evenly as possible.

Step 5.   Explain the Baker Street Rules for each *small group*:

1. Organize your group as you please.
2. Be sure to share all your clues with your group.
3. You can share your clues only by reading them aloud and then talking about them with the group.
4. You may not swap clues or show them to anyone.
5. Each group must answer all five questions of the mystery. Any time that your group thinks it knows the correct answers, you may write them down and hand them to me. I will only tell you if the *set of answers* is correct or incorrect. Either you are right or wrong. *It's all or nothing*.

You may wish to post these rules on the wall or give a copy of them to each group.

Step 6.   Tell the participants, "Begin. Read your clues to yourself and then share them with your group when you are ready. With these clues your group can solve Sherlock's mystery."

Step 7.   Observe the groups at work and enforce the rules with the assigned observer/enforcer, if there is one. Take some notes about how the groups are proceeding organizationally and "detectively."

Step 8.   Keep a set of correct answers (see Figure 6-5) handy for quick consultation. When a group hands you its answers, you will be able to compare the two sets. Tell the group whether it is correct or incorrect. If the set is incorrect, do not indicate which ones or how many are wrong. Just ask the group to try again with a new set of answers. *Remember: It's all or nothing*.

Step 9.   Debrief. As you debrief, try to keep your role as discussion facilitator and paraphraser. Try not to "preach" to the group. Patience will pay off.

Sherlock Plant

1. Clay pot
2. Azalea
3. East window
4. Water exceedingly well
5. In bloom; pink flowers

Sherlock Dinosaur

1. Saurischian
2. *Tyrannosaurus Rex*
3. 100 million years ago
4. Carnivorous
5. Two feet

FIGURE 6-5. Solutions to Sherlock Plant and Sherlock Dinosaur.

Read "Points Raised by Activity" to alert yourself to the points that generally come out during the debriefing section. Do not try to force more points than the group is willing to initiate because the forced points probably will not be meaningful anyway. Keep the extra points in mind, note them, and raise them at another time to your faculty when you wish to relate evaluation to the teaching process and to supervision.

Note that there are many sample questions below. You will no doubt not need to ask every question since many of the points will come to the floor without solicitation. Ask only those questions you want to ask and need to ask in order to keep the discussion going.

Follow the debriefing strategy below so you can reap the benefits of this structured activity:

1. Shift into the debriefing session by simply and only saying something like, "Now let's talk about what happened."

2. Begin the discussion by encouraging the *participants to describe what happened*. Let them "ventilate." Without sufficient hard-face ventilation there will not be an adequate basis for making discoveries and drawing conclusions later on. This opening phase of the debriefing will loosen up the participants and get them talking, as it is very easy to talk on this concrete, nonthreatening level. Be sure to call on observers to give a report if you have used them (in Step 2). Ask such questions as: What was the first step you took toward solving the mystery? What helped you solve the mystery? Did you organize yourselves in a special way? Did someone take notes to help organize your progress? Did a leader emerge in your group? What problems did you encounter in collaborating in the solving of the mystery? What did you learn about plants (dinosaurs)? What process or processes did you use in arriving at a decision regarding the answers to the five questions? Did you act differently in any way in your group from the way you act regularly? How did you feel when you solved the mystery?

3. *Analyze the data and points of this structured activity.* Discuss what all the activity in the group means; discuss what the points of the activity are. Ask such questions as: Compare your group's activity with what you would and could do by yourself? How did you benefit from collaborating with other people? What led to the emergence (or nonemergence) of a leader in your group? How did you overcome the problem of having so many clues to the mystery that you couldn't remember them all at one time? What key ideas does this activity present to us? What do all of these points mean in terms of working toward a solution of a problem? How could you have improved your group's procedures?

4. *Examine the implications of this activity for teaching and supervision.* Ask such questions as: What parallels are there between what happened here in this Sherlock activity and our teaching? What parallels are there between what happened here in this Sherlock activity and our supervision? What applications do you see for us based on the points raised about cooperation, collaboration, and interdependence? In what ways can we collaborate more as a faculty?

5. *Summarize, generalize, conclude.* Tie the many points together—the messages, the parallels, the implications, and the applications. Do not assume that the participants will generalize and draw conclusions on their own without guidance. Ask such questions as: From all we have said and done, what conclusions do you draw from this activity? What can you say to summarize what we have done and said today with this Sherlock whodunit activity?

If you wish, you can do the summarizing in a different way. You can request the group to list some key ideas that have come forth during the debriefing discussion and to offer some generalizations based on these key ideas. This approach is effective since the generalizations grow immediately and directly from what the group says. You can initiate this approach by asking each person to complete whichever of the following sentence stems you feel is more appropriate:

Based on this activity, I realize about my role in teaching

that _____.

Based on this activity, I realize about my role in supervision

that _____.

Be sure to ask the group to read their completed sentences.

Step 10.   Move forward. Before leaving the Sherlock whodunit behind, structure the activity so that you launch yourself and the group into something new built on it. In this way, you bridge current activity with future activity while interest is high. You can build, perhaps, on one of the ideas raised in the summary part of your debriefing, especially if you utilized the alternative summary approach that specifically elicits what people have realized from the activity. (See "Applications" for further ideas.)

POINTS RAISED BY ACTIVITY

1.   *Collaborative interdependence leads to positive experiences which can be the basis for friendship.* Seating two or three people next to each other in a room or assigning them to work in the same building does not necessarily mean that these people will become friends. Proximity may be a factor in friendship or the liking of one person by another, but it is not enough. When people work together on common problems, they build up a store of experiences to share and talk about. This is so whether the problem began as a common one or as belonging to one person alone with the other assuming the role of co-solver. It is the working together in an active way that leads to shared experiences and interactive communication, and these are the important factors leading to understanding, liking, and befriending.

The problem to be solved in Sherlock is the assigned mystery. By assignment, everyone shares that problem and assumes it willingly. Although it is assigned rather than being natural (which is the very nature of a structured activity), it is enough to lead people to work together. The distribution of the clues among several people and the Baker Street Rules require interdependence in order to solve the mystery. It is not a passive or weak interdependence but an active and strong one that requires verbal communication and cognitive collaboration. Without this collaborative interdependence the participants cannot solve the mystery. The interdependent experiences, meanwhile, serve to draw people together and make them like each other. Indeed, the research on students in a racially tense area who collaborate on common problems bears this out.[3]

2.   *Participants who collaborate interdependently develop a sense of groupness and belongingness.* In addition to the friendships that may be created by people who work together solving a common problem, there develops a sense of groupness and belongingness among people so engaged. A group is much more than a mere collection of five people. For example, five passengers on a city bus in Chicago do not comprise a group. A group develops when people have some common interests and shared experience. Then, as a consequence of the sense of groupness, members of the group behave in a special way—showing heightened care and responsibility toward each other. Cooperative members are able to put themselves in another's role. Once again, this sense of group develops quickly amongst most participants in Sherlock due to the active interdependence in sharing clues and solving the mystery. It also develops in classrooms where collaborative interdependence is promoted.

3. *Viewing and using other people as learning resources helps in problem solving.* It is one thing to cooperate with someone else in solving a problem or even to ask for help from that person. It is quite another thing to view others as learning resources and to learn from them. This latter approach establishes a different mind-set, one that promotes interdependence while encouraging a growing sense of independence based on new learning. When you view someone as a person to learn from, you look for knowledge and skills you can make your own eventually. This learning resources approach is one that is promoted by the collaborative interdependence theme and rules of Sherlock. It appears immediately and influences the quality of the interaction among group members.

4. *When solving a problem, it is good to know that you have the support of others.* The support you receive from other people is helpful when you are engaged in problem solving. In this structured activity, the support comes from people who are engaged in solving the same problem you are. In other situations, support may come from people who are not working with you. In either case, support is helpful. Many times it is necessary because without a sense of support you might give up your efforts. Indeed, the research on teachers shows that more than anything else teachers want *support* from their superiors.

In Sherlock, the support which you receive stems from the role you play in the group. You have clues which others need and vice versa. You pay attention to each other as you exchange clues in order to solve the mystery. Being an integral part of the group—a needed member of it—provides support to you. It encourages you to continue your efforts.

5. *Arriving at a solution leads to improved self-esteem.* Succeeding in your task to solve the mystery leads you to feel good about yourself. Success breeds increased self-esteem, and this is needed by everyone. The need for self-esteem is considered as a basic human need by leading theorists on motivation theory. It matters not that you achieved success along with several other group members rather than working independently. (Is it ever possible to do anything totally on your own? Is it possible to be 100 percent independent—to solve a problem independently?) Since you contributed to the solution as a collaborating member of the group, the success is yours, and you rightly feel a sense of increased self-esteem.

6. *Learning can be fun and painless.* Learning need not be a drudgery, something you dislike because of the unpleasant experiences associated with it. Learning can be fun and enjoyable, especially if it is the means to something else. In this structured activity, participants learn about plants (dinosaurs) without even realizing it because they are busy using the clues to solve the mystery.

The Baker Street Rules require that participants read the clues aloud, requiring everyone to pay close attention. The repetition of reading and hearing, which flows from the seeking of clear relations among clues, leads to reinforced learning. In this way, there is substantive learning regarding the content of the clues along with the procedural learning evolving from an interactive experience in a group activity. Learning proceeds on these two levels simultaneously.

7. *Solving a problem with a known solution is different from solving a problem when you do not even know if a solution is possible.* When you present the Sherlock scenario and the clues to the participants, you imply that a solution is possible. Indeed, you explicitly tell them that you know the solution and upon request you will tell them whether their solution is correct or not. With this idea in mind, the group sets out to discover the correct answers to the five questions posed in the scenario. This is easier than the pursuit of a solution to a problem when you don't know if the problem is even solvable.

It is necessary to keep in mind that the problems you face in education are different in several significant ways from Sherlock. Your problems do not come labeled "Problem," nor do your problems come with five prepared questions to answer so that if you can correctly answer them you know that you have the solution. Furthermore, your problems do not arrive at your desk with a set of clues ready to be sorted and worked through deductively. Rather, your problems come in a different form, without preset questions and without a set of neat clues. You must formulate the questions that need to be answered, and then you must go about gathering the information that will lead you to a solution.

Even though your problems require more of you than this Sherlock whodunit activity does, the procedures are essentially the same. You must phrase some question, gather up some clues in interaction with others, examine the clues for their relevance to each other, seek the collaborative help of others, and propose a tentative solution to your problem. Then you assess the solution. If it does not appear to be working, you return to your information (clues) and work imaginatively until you create another tentative solution. Your problems are harder, but the points learned from Sherlock, which poses an easier problem, still apply. It is for this reason that this structured activity is beneficial.

8. *Interdependence fosters active listening and active talking by group members and vice versa.* In order to solve a problem together with someone else, you need to communicate in an *active* way. Active listening means that you listen with the intention of understanding the cognitive and emotional messages being sent. Active talking means that you listen to the particular person before you talk in recognition of the unique characteristics of that person as you know them. Active listening and talking mean paying attention to the other person. Because you are interdependent, there is a need for you to be an active communicator.

At the same time, because you are actively communicating you foster interdependence. The other person recognizes that you are paying attention and being supportive. This recognition leads to positive feelings, reciprocity, and further interaction. As the interaction proceeds, especially as you move toward a solution, a good sense of interdependence develops. One result feeds on the other and helps the other to grow.

9.   *In complex situations a leader emerges to guide the group in reaching needed solutions.* With complexity comes brain strain and the need for leadership. Some Sherlock whodunit groups find it possible to solve the mystery without anyone taking notes. Such groups, however, are in the minority. Most participants find that they cannot keep track of so many clues in their heads alone. They need to take notes, write down connections among clues, and indicate conclusions drawn from the clues. Furthermore, even the small number of people in the group creates enough complexity in the interaction to require at least one person to take some written notes. In addition, in most groups an informal leader emerges who steers the members in their task.

All the more so in the complex situation of educational supervision. Problems, as mentioned above, do not appear in neat packages. Rules for interaction are not clearly and explicitly established, and the number of people involved—directly or indirectly—demands an intricate web of interaction. In supervision, the complexity is real and apparent to everyone. For these reasons it is natural that there is a leader. This is a human way for things to develop, and it is unrealistic to believe that complex groups can function otherwise.

SUGGESTIONS AND COMMENTS

1.   Read through the entire activity, especially "Points Raised by Activity." This will help you to determine the direction in which you will guide the debriefing discussion. You can talk with teachers about collaborative interdependence within their classroom, emphasizing the advantages of devoting part of the daily or weekly time schedule to activities promoting this theme, or you can talk with teachers and supervisors about collaborative interdependence in supervision. You can emphasize the necessity of collaboration if you are to succeed in the complex task of teacher development and an improved school environment for student learning, or you can talk about both ideas since the two topics are clearly related to each other. Obviously, it depends on your situation with your faculty, and the choice of emphasis is yours.

2.   In choosing the scenario—Sherlock Plant or Sherlock Dinosaur—you use with your faculty, keep in mind that your faculty may want to use the same scenario with their students. Their use of Sherlock whodunit would be one good way for them to introduce their students to this approach to learning if they are not already employing it. If you do not like either of the two Sherlocks presented here, you can create your own scenario and clues. If you follow this route, study the two Sherlocks for guidance on the components of an effective scenario, set of questions, and set of clues.

3.   If you feel that you have too many clues, remove a few of them before putting them in the envelope for distribution. For Sherlock Plant you may remove several from Nos. 25 to 30 only. (That is, be sure to keep Nos. 1 to 24.) For Sherlock Dinosaur you may also remove several from Nos. 25 to 30 only. (That is, be sure to keep Nos. 1 to 24.) Do not remove other clues or you will cause serious trouble for the participants.

4.   If you realize that every group member will not receive the same number of clues and you would like to keep everyone even, you can request the group distributor to place leftover clues in the middle of the table. You can declare these clues to be public property clues—clues to be handled by everyone as the group sees fit in contrast to the private property clues which each person receives from the distributor. Or, you can declare that these clues belong as private property to whoever claims them from the center of the table. In any case each participant should have at least four clues as private property.

5. If you are pressed for time, you can shorten the solving time by removing some clues and/or declaring some clues as public property. However, be careful not to make solving the mystery so easy that there is no challenge for your faculty to work against. Once you become familiar with the scenarios and clues, you will be able to give hints *if* you wish to make the task easier and therefore shorter.

6. If you wish to make an easy mystery you can, in addition to removing some clues from Nos. 25 to 30, give out some common clues. You could, for example, *give everyone* a copy of Clue 1 and/or Clue 2. This is an especially good idea if you are doing this activity with a group of elementary students with whom you are demonstrating this approach. Clues 1 and 2 will help a young group to get going easily.

7. Generally, you can conduct this entire activity in about seventy-five minutes. If you have more time, you can proceed slowly, especially in Steps 8 and 9, solving and debriefing. If you have an abundance of time, do not make the task very easy. Allow the group to struggle somewhat with about five or six clues each. In any case, leave at least thirty minutes for debriefing and moving forward. These steps are important since they allow you to relate this activity to your particular situation.

8. If you are superintendent, for example, and do not feel comfortable leading this activity with your faculty, by all means ask someone else to lead it. Perhaps a curriculum coordinator or department chair will lead this activity for you. You can be a participant or an observer, as you see fit.

APPLICATIONS

With its theme of collaboration and interdependence, this Sherlock whodunit activity clearly relates to supervision. Without promoting a commitment to collaboration and interdependence no supervisor can hope to succeed. A supervisor who somehow still believes that it is possible to succeed by unbending adherence to unilateral independence is simply doomed to a very difficult time and to poor odds for meaningful supervision. By definition supervision is interactive, and developmental supervision believes that you must build on what is natural rather than work in opposition to it. All sound supervision demands interdependence—a condition where the success of the teacher and success of the supervisor are positively correlated to each other.

SPECIAL MEMO

As with the other structured activities, one simple way to start a follow-up on the Sherlock activity is to send a memo to each person reminding the faculty of several key points raised and the suggestions made for future activity. Figure 6-6 offers an easy form to use as a quick and effective method for informing your faculty about your perspective on the training session. Your selection of quotable quotes and points raised will serve to let people know how you feel about the session.

TO: _____

FROM: _____

RE: Follow-up from Sherlock

  Led by _____ on _____, 19___

1. Quotable quotes from the session:

   A.

   B.

   C.

2. Key points raised:

   A.

   B.

   C.

3. Decisions to follow through for implementation:

FIGURE 6-6. Follow-up memo for Sherlock (blank).

TO: Intermediate Faculty

FROM: Thelma Kaelber

RE: Follow-up from Sherlock

Led by Ailene   on Sept. 30 , 19XX

1. Quotable quotes from the session:

    A. This was good for my brain to work out the "if" clues.

    B. I needed you and you needed me, and that was ideal. (Ted)

    C. Maryann: It just hit me that my philodendron is in the wrong window.

2. Key points raised:

    A. The success of our unit depends on contributions from everyone of us.

    B. Each of us can learn new techniques from someone else.

    C. If we want cooperative learning to take place in our classrooms, then it's up to us to set up the roles for it.

3. Decisions to follow through for implementation:

    At our meeting next week Ailene will present to us her experiences in group learning methods and some rules to follow in getting started. In the meantime please read a copy of the brief attached article on this matter by Slavin which you all requested from me. Come prepared to discuss the article which synthesizes the research and learn from Ailene.

FIGURE 6-7. Follow-up memo for Sherlock (filled in).

Figure 6-7 shows a completed form. You will note that the person sending the form is not the one who conducted the session. The points raised show that the total group began to consider themselves as a "unit," and that the teachers recognize their responsibility in bringing about change. Also, the group set up a further session involving peer teaching. Arlene will discuss her experiences with group collaborative learning. To keep them motivated, Thelma asks everyone to read an article by Robert Slavin,[4] which reviews and synthesizes the current research on this topic. (Slavin includes in his review the approach and research reported by Aronson, as mentioned in Point 1 in "Points Raised by Activity.")

SUPERVISION

When you meet with your faculty, either individually or in small groups, you have an excellent opportunity to raise the topic of collaborative interdependence. You can discuss ways for the teachers to include activities that are collaborative into their weekly schedules. The Sherlock and jigsaw approaches are but two; there are several others. The Slavin article is an excellent first step in searching for activities that require student cooperation in order to master the material to be learned. Particularly helpful is Slavin's set of references.

You can also talk about ways in which you and the faculty can collaborate. For example, you could conduct some action research together in the teacher's classroom. You could prepare a paper together for your local convention of supervisors based on your school's approach to supervision—on observations and conferences. There is an unlimited number of things you could collaborate on that will suit you. It is a matter of starting to think along these lines that is critical.

FACULTY MEETINGS AND COMMITTEES

The theme of collaborative interdependence pertains to faculty meetings as well. When the faculty grasps the sense and significance of interdependence, voting during meetings in terms of "we against them" will begin to disappear. As a faculty you are *one interdependent faculty*. It is, therefore, reasonable to mention this Sherlock activity at faculty meetings to remind people of their experiences during and after the activity. It probably is not necessary to do so in small committee meetings that concentrate on this task. It may not be possible to eliminate some of the splits among the faculty, but it is possible to smooth out the sharp edges and move closer to the recognition that faculty members must act together as one unit for the betterment of everyone concerned.

CONCLUDING WORDS

The Sherlock activity is a simple one with a familiar theme. Some people may tire of hearing about the importance of collaboration and interdependence. If so, the cause is not the triteness of the theme, but rather that people hear about it and talk about it without implementing it enough. Perhaps if the theme were more fully implemented in our schools we would not need to hear about it and talk about it explicitly so much.

Whatever the case, those of us who advocate developmental supervision focused on the growth of the teachers cannot afford to let up on our efforts to promote collaborative interdependence because it lies along the center of the route toward more effective schooling. Without the collaboration of teacher and supervisor the improvement of our schools cannot and will not occur because the pull in opposite directions has the net effect of impeding growth. The Sherlock activity highlights the fundamental reasons for collaborative interdependence: with it we can succeed; without it we will not be able to solve the problems facing us.

CHAPTER 6 ENDNOTES

1.   BEA MAYES and RONALD T. HYMAN, "Sherlock Plant," modified for this activity.

2.   JAN J. BIRD, "Sherlock Dinosaur," created by graduate student at Rutgers University to fit the Sherlock model.

3.   ELLIOT ARONSON et al., *The Jigsaw Classroom* (Beverly Hills, Calif: Sage Publications, 1978).

4.   ROBERT E. SLAVIN, "Synthesis of Research on Cooperative Learning," *Educational Leadership*, Vol. 38, No. 8 (May 1981): 655–660.

7	
	# *WINTER CRASH SURVIVAL* ## *Group Decision Making*

Winter Crash Survival is an excellent approach to help you and your faculty experience an alternative to the majority vote decision-making process. The activity teaches participants how to make decisions by consensus, which means that there is general agreement on an issue that everyone can support in some way. Consensus focuses on agreement, not win/lose or giving in. Participants learn how to decide by consensus as they decide how they will survive after a plane crash in winter.

After reading this chapter, you should be able to:

- Understand the purpose of, steps for, and points raised by the structured activity.
- Conduct Winter Crash Survival confidently with your faculty following the step-by-step strategy.
- Describe at least five points raised about decision making.
- List at least three guidelines for deciding by consensus.
- Know at least two ways to apply the points raised in the debriefing discussion with your faculty.

OVERVIEW

Winter Crash Survival[1] helps you to learn and practice the guidelines for working toward group consensus. (See Chapter 8 for more on using consensus in a faculty meeting.) Since many faculty activities occur in a small-group setting, which is ideal for utilizing the consensus approach to decision making, Winter Crash Survival offers an informative structured activity to use as the learning experience. Participants read a scenario about a plane crash, independently decide how they will act, and then decide again by reaching a consensus. In the debriefing session, participants discuss their experiences using two different approaches and compare the results.

MATERIALS NEEDED

Each participant needs a pencil, an eraser, and one copy each of the Individual Worksheet, the Group Worksheet, and the Record Sheet. You yourself need a copy of Background Information and Scoring Key.

NUMBER OF PARTICIPANTS

You need at least four people, although more is better. During the activity, you will divide the participants into small groups of four to seven people. The best size for a small group is five, but the size of each small group will, of course, depend on the total number of participants.

PROCEDURE

Step 1.   Introduce this activity *very briefly*. Simply ask the group to come along with you in an activity which will prove to be beneficial and enjoyable. Request their cooperation and be sure not to give away what will happen. The idea here is for the group to realize on its own what has happened when they debrief later in Step 13. So, say little and be brief in order to get things going.

Step 2.   Distribute the Individual Worksheet (Figure 7-1) for Winter Crash Survival. This sheet gives the scenario and the items saved from the crash.

Step 3.   Ask each person to read the sheet and correctly rank the items *independently*. Encourage people to jot down notes as they rank the fifteen items. If necessary, review the scenario with the group. Allow ten to fifteen minutes for this ranking. It may take a bit more time for a few people. Try not to rush them unless you are pressed for time. Remind them to work alone.

Step 4.   After all participants have finished ranking the fifteen items independently, ask the participants to form groups of four to seven people at most. Try to get groups of five, the best size for small group work. For example, if you have fourteen people, form two groups of five each and one group of four. Use your judgment here as to the number of groups and size of each group. You may find that to keep groups small it is helpful to ask one or two people to serve as observers during the group activity to follow. Observers will serve the function of providing an external source of data about what occurred in the various small groups. You will ask them to report later on. Ask them to take mental and written notes to help them later.

Step 5.   Distribute to each participant the Group Worksheet shown in Figure 7-2. Review this worksheet with the entire group, especially the four Guidelines for Decision Making by Consensus.

You have just crash-landed in the woods of North Minnesota and Southern Manitoba. It is 11:32 a.m. in mid-January. The small plane in which you were traveling has been completely destroyed except for the frame. The pilot and the copilot have been killed, but no one else is seriously injured.

The crash came suddenly before the pilot had time to radio for help or inform anyone of your position. Because your pilot was trying to avoid a storm, you know the plane was considerably off course. The pilot announced shortly before the crash that you were eighty miles northwest of a small town that is the nearest known habitation.

You are in a wilderness area made up of thick woods broken by many lakes and rivers. The last weather report indicated that the temperature would reach minus 25 degrees in the daytime and minus 40 at night. You are dressed in winter clothing appropriate for city wear—suits, pantsuits, street shoes, and overcoats.

You may assume that the number of survivors is the same as the number of people in your group and that the group has agreed to stick together.

While escaping from the plane your group salvaged the fifteen items listed here. Your task is to rank these items according to their importance to your group's survival, starting with "1" for the most important and proceeding to "15" for the least important:

A. _____ Compress kit (with 28 feet of 2-inch gauze)
B. _____ Ball of steel wool
C. _____ Cigarette lighter (without fluid)
D. _____ Loaded .45-caliber pistol
E. _____ Newspaper (one per person)
F. _____ Compass
G. _____ Two ski poles
H. _____ Knife
I. _____ Sectional air map made of plastic
J. _____ 30 feet of rope
K. _____ Family-size chocolate bar (one per person)
L. _____ Flashlight with batteries
M. _____ Quart of 85-proof whiskey
N. _____ Extra shirt and pants for each survivor
O. _____ Can of shortening

Used with permission of the authors, David W. Johnson and Frank P. Johnson.

FIGURE 7-1. Individual worksheet for Winter Crash Survival.

This is an exercise in group decision making for the Winter Crash Survival situation. Your group is to employ the method of group consensus to reach its decision. This means that the ranking for each of the 15 survival items must be agreed upon by each group member before it becomes a part of the group decision. Consensus is difficult to reach. Therefore, not every ranking will meet with everyone's complete approval. Nevertheless, try as a group to make each ranking one with which all group members can at least partially agree. Here are four Guidelines for Decision Making by Consensus:

1. Avoid arguing for your own individual judgments. Approach the task on the basis of reason.
2. Avoid changing your mind only to reach agreement and to avoid conflict. Support only decisions with which you are able to agree somewhat.
3. Avoid conflict-reducing techniques such as majority vote, averaging, or trading your decision.
4. View differences of opinion as helpful to, rather than as hindering, good decision-making.

Here are the 15 items:

A. _____ Compress kit (with 28 feet of 2-inch gauze)
B. _____ Ball of steel wool
C. _____ Cigarette lighter (without fluid)
D. _____ Loaded .45-caliber pistol
E. _____ Newspaper (one per person)
F. _____ Compass
G. _____ Two ski poles
H. _____ Knife
I. _____ Sectional air map made of plastic
J. _____ 30 feet of rope
K. _____ Family-size chocolate bar (one per person)
L. _____ Flashlight with batteries
M. _____ Quart of 85-proof whiskey
N. _____ Extra shirt and pants for each survivor
O. _____ Can of shortening

FIGURE 7-2. Group worksheet for Winter Crash Survival.

Step 6. Request participants to follow the Guidelines as they rank the fifteen items again by group consensus. Each person should fill out a sheet listing the group's decisions to refer to later. Obviously, each sheet in a small group will have the same rankings. Allow twenty to thirty minutes for this activity.

Step 7. When every group is finished with the Group Worksheet, distribute to every participant the Record Sheet (see Figure 7-3).

Step 8. Ask everyone to copy into Column III his or her rankings from the Individual Worksheet.

Step 9. Ask everyone to compute his or her individual score in Column II. The score is the absolute difference between the correct ranking (Column IV) and the person's individual ranking (Column III). Just subtract Column III from Column IV or vice versa and forget plus or minus signs. Write the answer in Column II to get the individual score. For example, if for Item H (Knife) a person has a ranking of six, then the score is four because the correct ranking is ten. Similarly, if for Item H the ranking is fourteen, the score is still four. That is, in either case the person has placed Item H (Knife) four ranks away from the correct ranking, and so the score for that item is four.

Step 10. When all participants are finished computing their individual scores, ask them to follow a similar procedure for computing the group score on the right side of the Record Sheet. That is, copy the group rankings into Column V and then subtract Column V from Column IV or vice versa to get the group score for Column VI.

Step 11. When all participants are finished computing the group score, ask them to compute the group's average individual score and the range of individual scores by filling in the bottom part of the Record Sheet.

Step 12. If you wish more data to help you in the debriefing which follows, ask each group to compute several other things: number of individual scores higher than the group score; number of individual scores lower than the group score; number of individual scores the same as the group score; total number of points higher than the group score; total number of points lower than the group score (see Figure 7-4).

Step 13. Debrief. As you debrief, try to keep your role as discussion facilitator and paraphraser. Try not to "preach" to the group. Patience will pay off.

Read through the section "Points Raised by Activity" to alert yourself to the points that generally come out during the debriefing section. Do not try to force more points than the group is willing to initiate because the forced points probably will not be meaningful anyway. Keep the extra points in mind, note them, and raise them at another time to your faculty when you wish to relate decision making to consensus.

Note that there are many sample questions below. You will no doubt not need to ask every question since many of the points will come to the floor without solicitation. Ask only those questions you want to ask and need to ask in order to keep the discussion going.

Follow the debriefing strategy below so you can reap the benefits of this structured activity.

1. Shift into the debriefing session by simply and only saying something like, "Now let's talk about what happened so far."
2. Begin the discussion by encouraging the *participants to describe what happened*. Let them "ventilate." Without sufficient hard-fact ventilation there will not be an adequate basis for making discoveries and drawing conclusions later on. This opening phase of

I	II	III	IV	V	VI
Item	My Individual Score	My Individual Ranking	Correct Ranking	My Group Ranking	My Group Score
A			11		
B			2		
C			1		
D			9		
E			8		
F			15		
G			12		
H			10		
I			14		
J			7		
K			4		
L			6		
M			13		
N			3		
O			5		
TOTAL					

My Individual Score ←   My Group Score →

} Individual Scores of others in my group

+ _____

{ Grand total of all Individual Scores, including my own, in my group

{ Average Individual Score (Grand Total ÷ number of people in my group, including myself)

Range of Individual Scores in my group is from a low score of [   ]

to a high score of [   ]

FIGURE 7-3. Record sheet for Winter Crash Survival.

Copy or derive the following data from your Record Sheet:

A. Range of Individual Scores—low to high	
B. Average Individual Score	
C. Group Score	
D. Number of people in group	
E. Number of Individual Scores higher than Group Score	
F. Number of Individual Scores lower than Group Score	
G. Number of Individual Scores same as Group Score	
H. Total of points of people in Item E above	
I. Total of points of people in Item F above	
J. Average of Item H above (H ÷ E)	
K. Average of Item I above (I ÷ F)	

FIGURE 7-4. Additional group data for Winter Crash Survival.

the debriefing will loosen up the participants and get them talking, as it is very easy to talk on this concrete, nonthreatening level. *Be sure to call on observers to give a report* if you have used them (in Step 4). Ask such questions as: How did you go about ranking the fifteen items—from fifteen to one or one to fifteen or mixed procedure? How did you feel working alone compared with working within your small group as you ranked the fifteen items? What are your individual scores? Your group scores? Your average individual scores? Your range of scores?

Put these data on the chalkboard or big easel pad or overhead projector for everyone to see. Simply ask each group to give you the data from the Group Worksheets as you fill in Figure 7-5 for the entire group, or the parts of Figure 7-5 with which you wish to work.

What item did you rank first? Last? What reasons did you give for your rankings when you talked in your group? (For information on reasons for the rankings, see Figure 7-9, Background Information and Scoring Key, at the end of this chapter. Supply that information to participants as they request it or talk about why each item is important for survival.)

3. *Analyze the data and the points of this structured activity.* Discuss what all the activity and information in the charts add up to; discuss what the points of this activity are. Ask such questions as: How do the individual scores compare with the average individual scores and the group scores? What do these data mean? What key ideas does this Winter Crash Survival activity present to us? What did you learn about yourself as you conferred within your group according to the Guidelines for Decision Making by Consensus as given to you on the Group Worksheet? What does this activity teach us?

4. *Examine the implications of this activity for teaching and supervision.* Ask such questions as: What parallels are there between our behavior in Winter Crash Survival and our teaching? What parallels are there between our behavior in Winter Crash Survival and our behavior as a faculty—in meetings and in supervision? What applications do you see for us based on the points you have raised? In what ways can we change our classroom behavior, and our faculty meeting behavior, and our supervisory behavior as a result of what we have learned from this activity? In what ways can we modify our behavior so we can utilize consensus as an alternative approach to decision making?

5. *Summarize, generalize, conclude.* Tie the many points together—the messages, the parallels, the implications, and the applications. Do not assume that the participants will generalize and draw conclusions on their own without guidance. Ask such questions as: From all that we have said and done, what conclusions do you draw from this activity? What can you say to summarize what we have done and said today with Winter Crash Survival?

    If you wish, you can do the summarizing in a different way. You can request the group to list some key ideas that have come forth during the debriefing discussion and to offer some generalizations based on these key ideas. This approach is effective since the generalizations grow immediately and directly from what the group says. You can initiate this approach by asking each person to complete whichever of the following sentence stems you feel is more appropriate:

    Based on this activity, I realize about teaching that _____

    _____.

	Group			
	1	2	3	4
A. Range of Individual Scores—low to high				
B. Average Individual Score				
C. Group Score				
D. Number of people in group				
E. Number of Individual Scores higher than Group Score				
F. Number of Individual Scores lower than Group Score				
G. Number of Individual Scores same as Group Score				
H. Total of points of people in Item E above				
I. Total of points of people in Item F above				
J. Average of Item H above (H ÷ E)				
K. Average of Item I above (I ÷ F)				

FIGURE 7-5. Additional group data for Winter Crash Survival.

Based on this activity, I realize about our faculty that _____
_____.

Be sure to ask the group to read their completed sentences.

Step 14. Move forward. Before leaving the Winter Crash Survival behind, structure the activity so that you launch yourself and the group into something new built on it. In this way, you bridge current activity with future activity while interest is high. You can build, perhaps, on one of the ideas raised in the summary part of your debriefing, especially if you have utilized the alternate summary approach which specifically elicits what people have realized from the activity. (See "Applications" for further ideas.)

POINTS RAISED BY ACTIVITY

It may be somewhat difficult for you as you read through this description of Winter Crash Survival to realize just what people will say during small group conferences and the debriefing. To help you, below are seven essential points that generally arise during this activity. You may find some others as well. By familiarizing yourself with these points, you will know what to expect and also be able to see how this activity can help you with your faculty. There is some overlap among the points that follow, but that is to be expected since they all stem from just one activity. In any case, each is worthy of mention.

1. *Consensus is an effective decision making process.* The realization of this point is the aim of Winter Crash Survival. If the data your group generates do not bear this out, you are in an unfortunate position. The data I have seen which show what other groups have done with similar scenarios bear out this point about the effectiveness of consensus. The data I have received from the *many, many* times I have personally used the Winter Crash Survival and its parent scenario, Lost on the Moon (a scenario about a NASA space rendezvous), all support this point 100 percent: Consensus is effective. Each time I have used this activity, no matter which scenario I have used, the group scores have been better (that is, lower) than the average individual scores and, with only one or two exceptions, better than the best individual score in the small group. Others who have used this activity report exactly the same conclusion.

Figure 7-6 gives data from one group of 14 department heads and administrators of one school. Note that for each small group of four or five members: (a) the group score is lower (that is, lower equals better because there is less divergence from the correct answer) than each member's individual score; and (b) the group score is lower than the average individual score. That is, while the best persons in the groups talked with the others in their groups, they improved even though the others had worse individual scores. Of course, at the time no one knew the "scores" but the rankings were already made. For example, in Group 3, the person with an individual score of 100 helped his (it was a "he") group achieve a score of forty-four. He talked with everyone in the group, including the person with a score of forty-nine, the lowest individual score in that group. As a result of the discussion following the consensus rules, all individuals lowered their

	Group 1	2	3	4
A. Range of Individual Scores—low to high	53–80	60–78	49–100	
B. Average Individual Score	66	68.5	68.4	
C. Group Score	42	50	44	
D. Number of people in group	5	4	5	
E. Number of Individual Scores higher than Group Score	5	4	5	
F. Number of Individual Scores lower than Group Score	0	0	0	
G. Number of Individual Scores same as Group Score	0	0	0	
H. Total of points of people in Item E above	122	74	110	
I. Total of points of people in Item F above	0	0	0	
J. Average of Item H above (H ÷ E)	24.4	18.5	22	
K. Average of Item I above (I ÷ F)	0	0	0	

FIGURE 7-6. Illustrative data for Winter Crash Survival.

scores to 44, which is their group score. In short, the person with the worst score helped the person with the best score and vice versa; they *all* helped each other. Indeed, in that group of five persons the total number of points gained (Item H) was 110, with no points lost.

In Group 1, while the range of individual scores was less than the range for Group 3 (a range of twenty-seven compared to a range of fifty-one) and the worst individual score was only eighty, the total number of points gained was 122. The average individual improvement from the individual scores to the group score was 24.4. Moreover, here the group score went down to forty-two. Even Group 2, with the narrowest range of individual scores and the lowest of the three worst individual scores, had an average individual improvement of 18.5. In every instance of my experience every small group has had a better score on Item H (improvement) than Item I (loss).

Such data are amazing! With the exception of perhaps one person in a large group scoring lower than his/her small group's group score—and then only by one to three points—these data are similar to what I have received each time I have used this activity with faculty. Jay Hall,[2] the originator of this type of activity with his scenario Lost on the Moon, uses the word "synergy" to describe this "happy event" of the group outperforming its own best individual. The synergy comes from people talking together in a special way. This leads to the next point.

2. *There are guidelines to follow in using the consensus approach.* It is not sufficient for people in small groups just to talk together. Rather, it is necessary that they talk in a certain way. That is, people should know the rules for talking in a manner which elicits positive exchanges and should also know that everyone in the group expects the others to talk that way. The guidelines which you have on the Group Worksheet summarize and provide the needed rules for helping people to talk together in a helpful way. The guidelines consist of some "do's" and "don't's," and have meaning in light of the introduction to them at the top of the Group Worksheet. Experience shows that these guidelines are effective.

3. *Training with these guidelines for deciding by consensus helps.* Several researchers, including Hall, have shown that groups which follow the guidelines do in fact do better than those groups which are not trained. When people learn the guidelines, by reading them and clarifying them with the group leader, they come to expect a different group atmosphere from what exists in other aspects of their lives. The new expectation is of a group where threat to the individual is low, and such a group is conducive to positive exchanges and learning. Hall put it nicely this way, "Ludicrous ineffective solutions to problems are the product of groups that are pessimistic about their own potential, and have imperfect ways of dealing with conflict. The horse that is put together by a committee that understands group dynamics won't turn out to be a camel: it may be a thoroughbred filly fit for the Triple Crown."[3]

When a group uses the consensus approach, the threat to the individual is low in social and psychological terms because there is no winning or losing in the group. Everyone is accepted for what he can contribute, and there is no arguing, per se, but talk about the best solution with differences of opinion accepted and valued. With an expectation of a low threat, people change their behavior, and a positive cycle of changed behavior influencing further changes in attitude occurs. People following the guidelines implicitly comprehend the positive atmosphere and proceed down the road to success.

Groups which do not follow such guidelines (that is, they haven't been trained with the instructions on the Group Worksheet and with personal clarifications) proceed to talk in ways which are familiar but negative and ineffective. One researcher[4] showed that "trained" groups did 40 percent better than the "untrained" groups. The data on the value of training are convincing in my view; therefore, I have chosen always to do this activity with "trained" groups so that everyone can begin to utilize the guidelines toward a positive approach to group talk.

4. *Reaching a consensus takes time.* It takes time for a group of people—even a small group of four to six people—to talk through a problem situation. When a trained group follows the guidelines, time flies. The positive atmosphere encourages active talking and listening and discourages dominating, interrupting, passivity, and sulking. In terms of the *short run*, consensus is inefficient. Only in the short run, however. That is, it takes longer to reach a first decision by consensus than it does by delegation or majority vote.

In the long run, however, consensus is not inefficient and may not take much time. Once the group members learn the guidelines and abide by them, feel comfortable with their group, and trust this approach to decision making, it is possible to make further decisions rapidly because people know how to proceed and are willing to get to the core of the issue in order to arrive at a solution.

The expectation that the group will follow the guidelines reduces uncertainty about the behavior of others. This reduced uncertainty leads to increased communication, which leads to improved exchange of information and beliefs. The net result of all of this is an increase in the pooling of resources, or to put it another way, in the efficiency of the group.

5. *Consensus works best when every group member is involved.* It is possible, of course, for consensus to take place when one or two members of the group hardly contribute to the group discussion. Such people may easily agree to items in order to reduce the time spent in discussion and also to reduce conflict. Nevertheless, such reductions do not benefit the group in the long run because the group lacks the benefit of the contributions of these quiet people. The group benefits when each person contributes as a resource so as to increase the pool of knowledge, skills, and beliefs from which the group can reach a solution to the issue before it. Quiet, passive group members impede the group's progress even though they are not disturbing it on the surface.

6. *Consensus is a powerful decision making process.* Using the consensus approach provides a distinct challenge to the group. It is harder to decide by consensus than by delegation or majority vote. This challenge makes the success gained ultimately even more satisfying. When the group task is hard, but not unreasonably so, the members stretch themselves more, have more positive feelings about the group and themselves, and give higher evaluations to the group. When they fail on a difficult task, group members do not feel as dissatisfied as they do when they fail on an easy task.

The power of the consensus process also derives from the fact that each member has a commitment to the solution. Each member has contributed to the solution and has agreed to it. There are no winners and no losers. This is quite different from the situation created when five people out of nine vote yes and four vote no in a group using a majority vote to decide an issue. It is certainly more powerful when everyone can say yes to an issue in some important way. The instructions on the Group Worksheet recognize that not every decision "will meet with everyone's complete approval." Nevertheless, an agreement by everyone in some way leads to a stake in the solution created.

   7. *Consensus is all the more important in situations where there is no "correct" solution.* In this Winter Crash Survival activity there is a correct solution offered by the creator of the activity. We use that solution to score our rankings. But in most of our lives, especially in the situations we face as faculty members, there are no correct solutions we can consult in order to see how well we are doing.

   In general, we do not have objective, external measures available to us. For this very reason we need to take steps that will maximize our communication with each other so we can benefit from all the resources available. A group which doesn't maximize its use of its own resources cannot be as effective as it might be. Increased communication within a positive environment and increased commitment to the decisions of the group toward solidarity in achieving the group's goals are essential to our functioning because we lack externally correct criteria. Consensus offers an approach with which groups can manage the natural conflicts that arise among people. By using the consensus method, groups can proceed toward creative, acceptable solutions to the problems they inevitably face.

SUGGESTIONS AND COMMENTS

   1.   Read through the entire activity, including the background information and scoring section. Participants may question why an item is ranked as it is. In responding, read or carefully cite the material provided by the activity's designers.

   2.   If you don't like this particular scenario you can use Lost on the Moon, the "parent" of Winter Crash Survival. Though Lost on the Moon is a bit out of date now, it is still highly effective. Or, you might wish to design your own scenario and items. If you do, be sure that you have an authoritative scoring key and rationale. In any case, conduct the activity as suggested here.

   3.   You can conduct this entire activity in about seventy-five to ninety minutes. If you have more time, then you can go slowly and easily use up two hours. If you must speed up, allow only twenty to thirty minutes in Step 6, group ranking. Circulate among the small groups and urge them to proceed more rapidly because of time restraints. Speed up in the individual ranking and the scoring. But leave at least thirty minutes for Steps 13 and 14, the debriefing and moving forward. These steps are most important since they bring home the message.

   4.   If you are a principal, for example, and do not feel comfortable leading this activity with your faculty, by all means ask someone else to lead it. Perhaps a particular guidance counselor, department chairperson, assistant principal, or senior faculty member is an excellent person to be the leader. You can be a participant or observer, as you see fit.

APPLICATIONS

Obviously, the Winter Crash Survival activity is not an end in itself. Its purpose is to teach the guidelines for reaching a decision by consensus and to encourage people to use these guidelines as they face problems in their groups. For this reason, it is necessary to build on the experience using Winter Crash Survival. You can direct the application to general faculty affairs or to smaller groups, committees or departmental faculties. In either case, you can easily build on this activity because the points raised apply to both levels of grouping of faculty.

SPECIAL MEMO

One simple way to follow up on Winter Crash Survival is to send a memo to each person, reminding the faculty of the points raised and suggestions made for future use. Figure 7-7 offers an easy form to use as a quick and effective method for informing your faculty about your perspective on the training session. Your selected quotations and points will let your faculty know how you feel about what happened.

Figure 7-8 shows a completed memo in which the English department chairperson, Lois, uses three brief quotations to show what struck her as important from the Winter Crash Survival. The first one, by George, is common: people have a tough time believing that a group can do better than the best individual person. As an English department chairperson, Lois shows that communication among faculty is important, even without adding the concept of consensus. That is, the four guidelines are good for communication in general, which is a concern of this department.

Finally, the group has decided to practice separately before implementing the guidelines during the next meeting. The group, in recognition of the results of the training session, has decided to act positively.

FACULTY MEETING

As you plan the agenda for the next faculty meeting, try to include and indicate one item which you believe should be decided by consensus rather than majority vote. Prepare a sheet with the guidelines for distribution at the meeting as you remind everyone of the training session guidelines.

The question, of course, is "What do we do when we have twenty-five people?" That is generally the first question asked by faculty who, though convinced of the merits of consensus, find it difficult to imagine using it in a group larger than ten. Yes, it is more difficult to reach consensus when the size of the group precludes easy and frequent exchanges among people. Nevertheless, it is possible to use consensus. First, no matter what the size of the group, you should remind everyone of the requirement to follow the consensus guidelines they have already learned as they consider the proposal before them. Second, do not entertain a motion that will set the tone for a majority vote procedure. Request that each person seek to understand the proposal clearly and to help the group work to consensus. The expectation and goal of reaching consensus should help.

TO: _____

FROM: _____

RE: Follow-up from Winter Crash Survival

    Led by _____ on _____, 19___

1. Quotable quotes from the session:

    A.

    B.

    C.

2. Key points raised:

    A.

    B.

    C.

3. Decisions to follow through for implementation:

FIGURE 7-7. Follow-up memo for Winter Crash Survival (blank).

TO: English Department Faculty

FROM: Lois

RE: Follow-up from Winter Crash Survival

    Led by   me   on Oct. 5 , 19XX

1. Quotable quotes from the session:

   A. George: I never would have believed it; I'd have bet against it any day.

   B. Hank: I learned one thing: if I ever crash in Minnesota, I want Evelyn with me.

   C. Evelyn: Hank is stubborn but he sure made us think through each item; that Floridian was actually helpful in the North.

2. Key points raised:

   A. Consensus takes time but it's worth it.

   B. A little bit of training and a commitment to follow the guidelines go a long way to improving communication.

   C. We all must be involved in our departmental decisions.

3. Decisions to follow through for implementation:
   We agreed to practice following the guidelines individually so that we'll be even more comfortable with them at our next department meeting. We'll try it at our meeting on October 12, on "Texts for the A.P. class."

FIGURE 7-8. Follow-up memo for Winter Crash Survival (filled in).

Note: None of the information here should be given to participants until after they have completed the decision making parts of the exercise.

Mid-January is the coldest time of the year in Minnesota and Manitoba. The first problem the survivors face, therefore, is to preserve their body heat and protect themselves against its loss. This problem can be met by building a fire, minimizing movement and exertion, and using as much insulation as possible.

The participants have just crash-landed. Many individuals tend to overlook the enormous shock reaction that has upon the human body, and the death of the pilot and copilot increases the shock. Decision-making under such conditions is extremely difficult. Such a situation requires a strong emphasis upon the use of reasoning, not only to make decisions, but also to reduce the fear and panic every person would naturally feel. Along with fear, shock reaction is manifested in feelings of helplessness, loneliness, and hopelessness. These feelings have brought about more fatalities than perhaps any other cause in survival situations. Through the use of reasoning, hope for survival, and the will to live can be generated. Certainly the state of shock means that movement of individuals should be at a minimum and that an attempt to calm them should be made.

Before taking off a pilot always has to file a flight plan. The flight plan contains the vital information regarding the flight, such as the course, speed, estimated time of arrival, type of aircraft, number of people on board, and so on. Search-and-rescue operations would begin shortly after the plane failed to arrive at its destination at its estimated time of arrival.

The 80 miles to the nearest known town is a very long walk even under ideal conditions, particularly if one is not used to walking such distances. Under the circumstances of being in shock, dressed in city clothes, having deep snow in the woods, and a variety of water barriers to cross, to attempt to walk out would mean almost certain death from freezing and exhaustion. At the temperatures given, the loss of body heat through exertion is a very serious matter.

Once the survivors have found ways in which to keep warm, their most immediate problem is to provide signaling methods to attract the attention of search planes and search parties. Thus, all the items the group has must be assessed according to their value in signaling the group's whereabouts.

The correct ranking of the survivors' items was made on the basis of information provided by Mark Wanig and supplemented from *The New Way of the Wilderness*, by C. Rutstrum (New York: Collier, 1973). Wanig was an instructor for three years in survival training in the reconnaissance school in the 101st Division of the U. S. Army and later an instructor on wilderness survival for four years at the Twin City Institute for Talented Youth. He is now conducting wilderness-survival programs for Minneapolis teachers.

Rank 1. *Cigarette lighter (without fluid)*. The gravest danger facing the group is exposure to cold. The greatest need is for a source of warmth, and the second greatest need is for signaling devices. This makes building a fire the first order of business. Without matches something is needed to produce sparks to start a fire. Even without fluid the cigarette lighter can be used to produce sparks. The fire will not only provide warmth, it will also provide smoke for daytime signaling and firelight for nighttime signaling.

FIGURE 7-9. Background information and scoring key for Winter Crash Survival.

Rank 2. *Ball of steel wool*. To make a fire, a means of catching the sparks made by the cigarette lighter is needed. Steel wool is the best substance with which to catch a spark and support a flame, even if it is a little bit wet.

Rank 3. *Extra shirt and pants for each survivor*. Clothes are probably the most versatile items one can have in a situation like this. Besides adding warmth to the body they can be used for shelter, signaling, bedding, bandages, string when unraveled, and tinder to make fires. Maps can even be drawn on them. The versatility of clothes and the need for fires, signaling devices, and warmth make this item number three in importance.

Rank 4. *Family-size chocolate bar (one per person)*. To gather wood for the fire and to set up signals, energy is needed. The chocolate bars would supply the energy to sustain the survivors for quite some time. Because they contain basically carbohydrates, they would supply energy without making digestive demands upon the body.

Rank 5. *Can of shortening*. This item has many uses—the most important being that a mirrorlike signaling device can be made from the lid. After shining the lid with the steel wool, the survivors can use it to produce an effective reflector of sunlight. A mirror is the most powerful tool they have for communicating their presence. In sunlight, a simple mirror can generate 5 to 7 million candlepower. The reflected sunbeam can be seen beyond the horizon. Its effectiveness is somewhat limited by the trees, but one member of the group could climb a tree and use the mirror to signal search planes. If the survivors have no other means of signaling, they would still have a better than 80 percent chance of being rescued within the first 24 hours.

Other uses for the item are as follows: Shortening can be rubbed on the body to protect exposed areas, such as the face, lips, and hands, from the cold. In desperation it could be eaten in small amounts. When melted into oil, shortening is helpful in starting fires. Melted shortening, when soaked into a piece of cloth, will produce an effective candlewick. The can is useful in melting snow to produce drinking water. Even in the winter, water is important as the body loses water in many ways such as perspiration, respiration, shock reactions, and so on. This water must be replenished because dehydration affects the ability to make clear decisions. The can is also useful as a cup.

Rank 6. *Flashlight with batteries*. Inasmuch as the group has little hope of survival if it decides to walk out, its major hope is to catch the attention of search planes. During the day the lid-mirror, smoke, and flags made from clothing represent the best devices. During the night the flashlight is the best signaling device. It is the only effective night-signaling device besides the fire. In the cold, however, a flashlight loses the power in its battery very quickly. It must therefore, be kept warm if it is to work, which means that it must be kept close to someone's body. The value of the flashlight lies in the fact that if the fire burns low or inadvertently is allowed to go out, the flashlight could be immediately turned on the moment a plane is heard.

Rank 7. *30 feet of rope*. The rope is another versatile piece of equipment. It could be used to pull dead limbs off trees for firewood. When cut into pieces, the rope will help in constructing shelters. It can be burned. When frayed it can be used as tinder to start fires. When unraveled it will make good insulation from the cold if it is stuffed inside clothing.

Figure 7-9 (continued)

Rank 8. *Newspaper (one per person)*. The newspaper could be used for starting a fire in much the same way as the rope. It will also serve as an insulator; when rolled up and placed under the clothes around a person's legs or arms, it provides dead-air space for extra protection from the cold. The paper can be used for recreation by reading it, memorizing it, folding it, or tearing it. It could be rolled into a cone and yelled through as a signal device. It could also be spread around an area to help signal a rescue party.

Rank 9. *Loaded .45-caliber pistol*. This pistol provides a sound-signaling device. (The international distress signal is three shots fired in rapid succession.) There have been numerous cases of survivors going undetected because by the time the rescue party arrived in the area the survivors were too weak to make a loud enough noise to attract attention. The butt of the pistol could be used as a hammer. The powder from the shells will assist in fire building. By placing a small bit of cloth in a cartridge, emptied of its bullet, a fire can be started by firing the gun at dry wood on the ground. At night the muzzle blast of the gun is visible, which also makes it useful as a signaling device.

The pistol's advantages are counterbalanced by its dangerous disadvantages. Anger, frustration, impatience, irritability, and lapses of rationality may increase as the group waits to be rescued. The availability of a lethal weapon is a real danger to the group under these conditions. Although a gun could be used for hunting, it would take a highly skilled marksman to kill an animal, and then the animal would have to be transported through the snow to the crash area, probably taking more energy than would be advisable.

Rank 10. *Knife*. A knife is a versatile tool, but it is not too important in the winter setting. It could be used for cutting the rope into desired lengths and making shavings from pieces of wood for tinder; many other uses could be thought up.

Rank 11. *Compress kit (with gauze)*. The best use for this item is to wrap the gauze around exposed areas of the body for insulation. Feet and hands are probably the most vulnerable to frostbite, and the gauze can be used to keep them warm. The gauze can be used as a candle wick when dipped into melted shortening. It would also make effective tinder. The small supply of the gauze is the reason this item is ranked so low.

Rank 12. *Two ski poles*. Although they are not very important, the poles are useful as a flagpole or staff for signaling. They can be used to stabilize a person walking through the snow to collect wood, and to test the thickness of the ice on a lakeshore or stream. Probably their most useful function would be as supports for a shelter or by the fire for a heat reflector.

Rank 13. *Quart of 85-proof whiskey*. The only useful function of the whiskey is to aid in fire building or as a fuel. A torch could be made from a piece of clothing soaked in the whiskey and attached to an upright ski pole. The danger of the whiskey is that someone might try to drink it when it is cold. Whiskey takes on the temperature it is exposed to, and a drink of it at minus thirty degrees would freeze a person's esophagus and stomach and do considerable damage to the mouth. Drinking it warm will cause dehydration. The empty bottle, kept warm, would be useful for storing drinking water.

Rank 14. *Sectional air map made of plastic*. This item is dangerous because it will encourage individuals to attempt to walk to the nearest town, thereby condemning them to almost certain death.

Figure 7-9 (continued).

Rank 15. *Compass.* Because the compass may also encourage some survivors to try to walk to the nearest town, it too is a dangerous item. The only redeeming feature of the compass is the possible use of its glass top as a reflector of sunlight to signal search planes, but it is the least effective of the potential signaling devices available. That it might tempt survivors to walk away from the crash site makes it the least desirable of the fifteen items.

*Used with permission of the authors David W. Johnson and Frank P. Johnson.

Figure 7-9 (continued)

Obviously, in the time available to you because you do not have unlimited time, you might not be able to say, for example, "I think that we have reached a consensus about the school trip: we'll have it Monday through Wednesday." But you can increase the opportunity as you move along if you "test the water" occasionally by asking for feedback on the distance faculty members are in their minds from coming to agreement. You can also take a *few* minutes to ask people to break into trios, quartets, or quintets to iron out a point or two. Finally when you believe you are as close to consensus as you might get in the given amount of time, you can be satisfied with less than a 100 percent agreement, which is much greater than a 51 percent majority. A near consensus achieved under good conditions is still better than a 51 percent majority where the "losing" minority is angry and not committed to the decision.

In short, consensus is not always possible, given the time available and the size of the group. Consensus is appropriate as one alternative to the ever-present majority vote. The Quakers, who seek a "sense of the meeting," have succeeded with the consensus approach for over 300 years now, showing that in large groups consensus is a viable approach to making a decision. Other groups also use the consensus approach successfully. It is possible to use consensus; much will depend on you as leader in terms of teaching and encouraging the use of the Guidelines for Decision Making by Consensus. This is true in a large group or a small group because the same rules apply, and the results are worth striving for in terms of group commitment and staff development.

CONCLUDING WORDS

Consensus is an approach to decision making which is not as often utilized as it might well be. Perhaps it is not as common as it might be because people simply don't know how to go about reaching consensus. Their current daily mode of interaction too often prevents them in groups from using consensus. Winter Crash Survival offers an excellent structured activity for learning the consensus perspective and the guidelines for decision making by consensus. The points often raised in the debriefing discussion demonstrate the power and importance of consensus.

CHAPTER 7 ENDNOTES

1. DAVID W. JOHNSON and FRANK P. JOHNSON, "Winter Survival," *Joining Together* (Englewood Cliffs, N.J.: Prentice-Hall, Inc., 1975), 318–321, 355.

2. JAY HALL, "Lost on the Moon" scenario, *Psychology Today* (November 1971): 51.

3. *Ibid.*, 88.

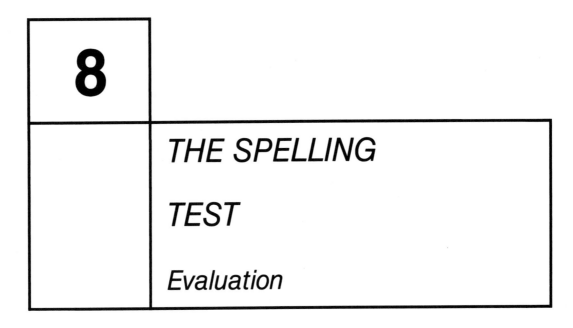

8

THE SPELLING

TEST

Evaluation

Participants in The Spelling Test have the opportunity to examine a persistent issue in education, namely, evaluation of someone else's performance. As a structured activity, The Spelling Test allows you to lead your faculty through an experience that is both enjoyable and enlightening because the simple required tasks raise questions that deserve answers. Yet, as in many areas of education, there are no absolute answers or formulas you can apply almost blindly so as to arrive at easily accepted positions.

After reading this chapter, you should be able to:

- Understand the purpose of, steps for, and points raised by The Spelling Test.
- Conduct The Spelling Test confidently with your faculty following the step-by-step strategy.
- List the four components of evaluation.
- Describe at least five persistent issues related to evaluation.
- Know at least two ways you can apply the points raised in the debriefing discussion to the supervision of your faculty.

OVERVIEW

Based on activities by B. Harris, W. Bessent, and K. McIntyre,[1] The Spelling Test, including the Arithmetic Test Item as a concluding supplemental alternative, offers you the opportunity to engage your faculty in a profitable discussion about evaluation. Evaluation of student performance and teacher performance is a persistent and complex issue in supervision. The specific issues within evaluation (for example, measurement) deserve attention and comment for they are at the center of the relationship between teacher and student as well as between supervisor and teacher. Participants in The

Spelling Test activity become involved in the evaluation issues when they score and grade a spelling test of a student named Janice Henry. In the debriefing session the participants discuss the standards they used in giving the student an A, B, C, D, or F grade. As they compare standards they raise other issues such as faculty fallibility. You can guide the participants toward a discussion of evaluation in supervision or evaluation in teaching or both, as your needs require. Each type of discussion will be of value to you in supervision.

MATERIALS NEEDED

Each participant needs a pen or pencil, a copy of Janice Henry's spelling test, and a copy of the Key to Spelling Test. Keep a dictionary available, but out of sight, until someone requests it. Also, if you use the Arithmetic Test Item mentioned in Point 4 of "Points Raised by Activity," you may want to have that reproduced on a sheet to be distributed to each person. However, even without a prepared sheet, you can still use it by quickly writing it on a chalkboard, overhead acetate, or easel pad.

NUMBER OF PARTICIPANTS

There is really no limit to the number of people who can participate in The Spelling Test at the same time. The minimum number is four so that you can have a group of people to raise evaluation issues and a group with whom you can discuss those issues.

PROCEDURE

Step 1.   Introduce this activity *very briefly*. Simply ask the group to join you in an activity which you believe is beneficial to all of you as will be evident in the ensuing discussion. Be sure not to reveal what will happen. The idea is for the group to realize on its own what has happened when they debrief in Step 9. So, say little and be brief in order to get the activity going quickly.

Step 2.   Distribute Janice Henry's test paper (see Figure 8-1) to everyone. Without giving any further information to the group, ask each person to score the test. Tell the participants that they are to score the test *individually and without any aids*; they are to use only their own knowledge. That is, which and how many words did Janice Henry spell correctly? Each records it as: Step A_____.

Step 3.   Distribute the Key to Spelling Test (Figure 8-2). Ask the participants to score Janice Henry's test again *individually and to use the key* this time. Which and how many words did Janice Henry spell correctly? Each records it as: Step B_____. If anyone challenges the scoring key, simply tell him or her that it is correct. If there is further challenge, offer the dictionary as a resource. If no one challenges anything, be silent and do not reveal that you have a dictionary available.

Step 4.   Ask each person *individually* to compute Janice Henry's percentage of correct words. Each records it as: Step C_____.

Name _Janice Henry_   Title _Spelling Test_

Class _Eng._   Period _3_

1. accommodate
2. aeronaltics
3. apparatus
4. beginning
5. cemetary
6. chauffer
7. complexion
8. consientious
9. cylinder
10. defense
11. decent
12. dessert
13. dicipline
14. ecstasy
15. embarass
16. exaggerated
17. foreign
18. grammer
19. grievous

20. height
21. interrupt
22. lieutenant
23. lovable
24. maintenance
25. mathmatics
26. mileage
27. mischevous
28. misspell
29. murmur
30. noticeable
31. nuisance
32. occurrance
33. original
34. pamphlet
35. parliament
36. personell
37. prejudice
38. priviledge
39. professor

40. psychology
41. reccommend
42. referred
43. restaurant
44. sacreligious
45. seize
46. seperate
47. similar
48. sophamore
49. therefore
50. they're
51. tobacco
52. unnecessary
53. vengance
54. yield

*Used with permission of Ben M. Harris.

FIGURE 8-1. Janice Henry's answers for The Spelling Test.*

1. accommodate	19. grievous	37. prejudice
2. aeronautics	20. height	38. privilege
3. apparatus	21. interrupt	39. professor
4. beginning	22. lieutenant	40. psychology
5. cemetery	23. lovable	41. recommend
6. chauffeur	24. maintenance	42. referred
7. complexion	25. mathematics	43. restaurant
8. conscientious	26. mileage	44. sacrilegious
9. cylinder	27. mischievous	45. seize
10. defense	28. misspell	46. separate
11. descent	29. murmur	47. similar
12. dessert	30. noticeable	48. sophomore
13. discipline	31. nuisance	49. therefore
14. ecstasy	32. occurrence	50. they're
15. embarrass	33. original	51. tobacco
16. exaggerated	34. pamphlet	52. unnecessary
17. foreign	35. parliament	53. vengeance
18. grammar	36. personnel	54. yield

*Used with permission of Ben M. Harris.
FIGURE 8-2. Key to The Spelling Test.*

Step 5. Ask each person *individually* to give Janice Henry a grade of A, B, C, D, or F. This is the grading system used by her school for the eighth grade. The school permits no plus (+) or minus (−) signs to be assigned. Do not give any further information to the group. If they ask for any guidance or criteria for a grade or for further information, tell them that they are to use their own criteria to grade Janice Henry's test which they have before them. Each records it as: Step D_____.

Step 6. Ask each person *individually* to give Janice Henry a grade of A, B, C, D, or F in light of information about her eighth-grade *class* (homeroom class) as follows:

Highest Score   —   41
Lowest Score   —   26
Average Score   —   33
Janice's score is one of the top four.
There are twenty-five students in her class.

Each records it as: Step E_____.

Step 7. Ask each person *individually* to give Janice Henry a grade of A, B, C, D, or F in light of information about her entire *school*. There are nine eighth-grade classes of 250 students total. All took the same test with the following results:

Highest Score   —   42
Lowest Score   —   0
Average Score   —   22
Janice's score is one of the top five.

Each records it as: Step F_____.

Step 8.   Ask the participants to form small groups of four to five members each. Ask them *together* to repeat the steps they have done individually: score the test (with the Key, Step B); compute the percentage of correct words (Step C); assign a grade with no further information about Janice Henry (Step D); assign a grade with information about the class (Step E); assign a grade with information about the school (Step F). You can leave the groups alone, or you can request that each group follow a particular approach in deciding which grade to assign Janice Henry in Steps D, E, or F. That is to say, you can: (1) give them no direction and thereby let them proceed in their own way to decide on a grade; (2) ask them to use majority vote, especially if you have formed them with an odd number of people in each group; (3) ask them to use consensus guidelines, as they have learned previously from Winter Crash Survival (see Chapter 7); (4) ask them to delegate a leader who will decide after hearing the group's discussion at each step; or (5) direct them to whichever other approach you decide on. In any case, ask them to come up with a group score, a group percentage, and three separate group grades in the time allotted to them so you can have material from each group for comparison.

You may wish to keep groups small and odd-numbered so as to avoid the possibility of a tie when using the majority vote approach. You can do this by assigning one or two people to be observers of the group discussions instead of being participants in the small groups. Observers will serve the good function of providing an external source of data about what occurred in the various small groups. You will ask them to report later on. Ask them to take mental notes and written notes to help them later.

Step 9.   Debrief. As you debrief, try to keep your role as discussion facilitator and paraphraser. Try not to "preach" to the group. Patience will pay off.

Read through "Points Raised by Activity" to alert yourself to the points which generally come out during the debriefing session. Do not try to force more points than the group is willing to initiate because the forced points probably will not be meaningful anyway. Keep the extra points in mind, note them, and raise them to your faculty at another time when you wish to relate evaluation to the teaching process and to supervision.

Note that there are many sample questions below. You will no doubt not need to ask every question since many of the points will come to the floor without solicitation. Ask only those questions you want to ask and need to ask in order to keep the discussion going.

Follow the debriefing strategy below so you can reap the benefits of this structured activity.

1.   Shift into the debriefing session by simply and only saying something like, "Now let's talk about what happened."

2.   Begin the discussion by encouraging the *participants to describe what happened.* Let them "ventilate." Without sufficient hard-fact ventilation there will not be an adequate

basis for making discoveries and drawing conclusions later on. This opening phase of the debriefing will loosen up the participants and get them talking, as it is very easy to talk on this concrete, nonthreatening level. Be sure to call on observers to give a report if you have used them (in Step 8). Ask such questions as: What *score* did you give Janice when you scored the test on your own and without the key (Step A)? What difficulties did you encounter in *scoring* the test? What score do you give Janice when you used the key to help you (Step B)? What was the percentage you computed (Step C)? Did you have any difficulty computing a percentage? What grades did you give Janice in Step D, Step E, and Step F? What were the results in your small group for Steps B, C, D, E, and F? Who scored the test correctly in Step A? In Step B?

Put these data on the chalkboard or easel pad or overhead projector for everyone to see. Simply ask each group to give you the data to fill out Figure 8-3 or the parts of Figure 8-3 with which you wish to work.

What criteria did you use in giving a grade to Janice Henry in Steps D, E, and F? Who changed grades after receiving more information? What information was critical in leading you to switch? What approach did your group use in deciding on grades? How did you feel about this? Did you use a dictionary? Did you trust the scoring key?

3. *Analyze the data and the points of this structured activity.* Discuss what all the activity and data in Figure 8-3 add up to; discuss what the points of the activity are. Ask such questions as: How do the individual scores and grades compare to the group scores and grades? How do your individual scores *without the key* (Step A) and your individual score *with the key* (Step B) compare? How do the grades shift from Step D—without any further information—to Step E—with class information—to Step F— with school information? Will the criteria for grading change if we grade another test,

	Group 1	Group 2	Group 3	Group 4
A. Range of Individual Scores Without Key (Step A)				
B. Range of Individual Scores With Key (Step B)				
C. Range of Percentages for Scores With Key (Step C)				
D. Range of Individual Grades for Step D				
E. Range of Individual Grades for Step E				
F. Range of Individual Grades for Step F				
G. Group Score With Key (Step B)				
H. Group Percentage (Step C)				
I. Group Grade for Step D				
J. Group Grade for Step E				
K. Group Grade for Step F				
L. Number of People in Group				

FIGURE 8-3. Individual and group data sheet for The Spelling Test.

for example, a social studies test? Math? English? Art? (See "Suggestions and Comments" for an interesting option at this point.) What do these data mean? What key ideas does this Spelling Test activity present to us? What did you learn about yourself as you scored and graded Janice Henry's test individually and in a group? How effective was your group process?

4. *Examine the implications of this activity for teaching and supervision.* Ask such questions as: What parallels are there between what happened here in The Spelling Test activity and our teaching? What parallels are there between what happened here in The Spelling Test activity and our supervision? What application do you see for us based on the points raised? In what ways can we change our scoring and grading procedures as a result of what we have learned from this activity?

5. *Summarize, generalize, conclude.* Tie the many points together—the messages, the parallels, the implications, and the applications. Do not assume that the participants will generalize and draw conclusions on their own without guidance. Ask such questions as: From all that we have said and done, what conclusions do you draw from this activity? What can you say to summarize what we have done and said today with this Spelling Test?

If you wish, you can do the summarizing in a different way. You can request the group to list some key ideas that have come forth during the debriefing discussion and to offer some generalizations based on these key ideas. This approach is effective since the generalizations grow immediately and directly from what the group says. You can initiate this approach by asking each person to complete whichever of the following sentence stems you feel is more appropriate:

Based on this activity, I realize about teaching and evaluating that _____

_____.

Based on this activity, I realize about supervising and evaluating that _____

_____.

Be sure to ask the group to read their completed sentences.

Step 10.   Move forward. Before leaving The Spelling Test behind, structure the activity so that you launch yourself and the group into something new built on it. In this way, you bridge current activity with future activity while interest is high. You can build, perhaps, on one of the ideas raised in the summary part of your debriefing, especially if you have utilized the alternative summary approach which specifically elicits what people have realized from the activity. (See "Applications" later in this chapter for further ideas.)

POINTS RAISED BY ACTIVITY

1.   *Evaluation is a complex process and requires criteria, but the criteria are not necessarily known to us or commonly agreed upon.* This point is not new or revolutionary; you have all heard this before. Nevertheless, this point comes forth strongly with a simple spelling test where you are not expecting difficulty. That is, you recognize that if there is complexity regarding evaluation of a cut-and-dry spelling test—where there are absolute standards for an item being correct or incorrect—then the matter of evaluation of other matters that are not measured so straightforwardly surely must be subjective. Indeed, the matter of evaluation is complex and subjective whether or not the activity being evaluated can be measured in terms that yield a precisely correct or incorrect result.

Valuing, then, begins where measurement, which is the prior step, ends, and it requires us to use criteria to determine whether the activity or person merits an A, B, C, D, or F. *Subjectivity enters because the criteria may not be clear to you or known to you explicitly*, even if they are personal criteria you are applying. Subjectivity also enters when there are external criteria that you must interpret and then apply on your own. The situation is further complicated when you expect or believe that there are external criteria but in fact there are no publicly agreed upon criteria.

For example, when you evaluate Janice Henry you don't have any public criteria for giving her an A, B, C, D, or F. You may believe that there are some criteria, but, in fact, there are no criteria which everyone agrees upon. You simply do not know on what common basis to give an A, B, C, D, or F. You fall back to your personal criteria, but these may not be clear to you, either. The assigning of a grade (that is, making an evaluation) requires you to consider Janice Henry's performance in light of your personal criteria, which you may not be fully aware of yourself regarding an eighth-grade spelling test. You are subjective, then, as you interpret the test score in light of your personal criteria. It is for this reason no doubt that the various people in your group arrived at different grades for Janice Henry. In Figure 8-4, showing illustrative data from a group of twenty-seven people, Rows D, E, and F show that individuals gave grades from D to B initially. Eventually the range was D to A.

2. *Evaluation is done within a context, and the context influences the evaluation given.* Evaluation, like everything else in the world, takes place within a context. This context includes the purpose of the activity being evaluated as well as the performances of other people in a similar situation. With this activity you don't know the purpose of the spelling test given to Janice Henry. Is it a pretest? Is it a posttest after a three-week unit on spelling demons? Is it a practice test for a standardized achievement test? Is it a practice test for screening applicants for the national spelling bee contest? Since you don't know the purpose of the test, you don't know how to interpret the data you have, thirty-seven correct out of fifty-four. (Indeed, the correct test score is thirty-seven.)

Furthermore, *in order to understand anyone's performance it is helpful to know how other people in a similar situation performed.* This is true whether that person is a student or a teacher, or whether you know the purpose of the activity or not. The question is: How well do others in a similar situation perform? So, for example, when you receive data about Janice Henry relative to her class, you must determine once again what her grade is. As shown in Row E of Figure 8-4, some people gave a different grade when evaluating Janice Henry with knowledge of her classmates' performances. Groups, as shown in Row J, also changed their minds. Group 1 switched from a D to a B, while Groups 3, 4, 5, and 6 raised Janice's grade only one level. On the other hand, Group 2 maintained its grade of D even though it received comparative data about Janice's class of twenty-five.

	Group 1	Group 2	Group 3	Group 4	Group 5	Group 6
A. Range of Individual Scores Without Key (Step A)	33-38	37-42	37-42	37-41	36-41	35-42
B. Range of Individual Scores With Key (Step B)	34-38	38-40	37-42	38-39	38-41	37-38
C. Range of Percentages for Scores With Key (Step C)	63-71%	67-76%	67-74%	70-71%	70-76%	69-71%
D. Range of Individual Grades for Step D	C-D	C-D	B-D	C-D	B-D	B-C
E. Range of Individual Grades for Step E	C-A	C-D	B	B-D	B	A-B
F. Range of Individual Grades for Step F	A-B	B-D	B	A-B	A	A-B
G. Group Score With Key (Step B)	37	37	37	37	37	37
H. Group Percentage (Step C)	69	69	69	69	69	69
I. Group Grade for Step D	D	D	C	C	C	C
J. Group Grade for Step E	B	D	B	B	B	B
K. Group Grade for Step F	A	D	B	B	A	A
L. Number of People in Group	4	4	4	5	5	5

FIGURE 8-4. Illustrative data for The Spelling Test from a group of twenty-seven people.

As shown in Row F and Row K, there was further change once people received data comparing Janice to an even larger group, the entire 250 students in eighth grade. Group 1 gave Janice an A at this point, a three-grade jump from D when there was no comparative information at all. Groups 3 and 4 maintained their grade of B; Groups 5 and 6 moved from a grade of B to an A; and Group 2 stayed with a B even though Janice Henry was one of the top five in her entire eighth grade. *All received the same information but interpreted it differently,* and this is natural and normal.

In short, the context of a situation influences your evaluation. People are influenced by the purpose of the activity and the comparative data available to them. Would those who gave Janice Henry a D still maintain that grade if (1) this test were a posttest after one week of study and (2) Janice, a mainstreamed special education student with minor brain retardation, had one week ago spelled only six correct on the pretest?

3. *Errors in measurement are common and to be expected.* Though we often consider measuring an easy skill, experience shows that measuring is indeed more complicated and open to error than we often realize. On this eighth-grade test, for example, the scoring (that is, measuring) of the number of words spelled correctly supposedly should be a simple, straightforward matter for a group of adults. Yet, only six people of the twenty-seven in the group which generated the data scored Janice Henry's test correctly without a key. What is more, only thirteen scored it correctly with the scoring key! (These data are not shown in Figure 8-4, but are known from the debriefing with the group.)

Since the words in the spelling test include some difficult words, or "demons," it is easy to understand why people made errors in scoring (see Figure 8-4, Row A). But you must reconsider any idea you had about the ease of measurement when you realize that even with the key in their hands, people make errors in scoring the test. We know this from the illustrative data by noting that in Row B, the range with the scoring key was from thirty-four to forty-two. In short, though people often focus on the assignment of a grade as the element which introduces differences among people, *measurement, usually considered to be an easy task, also introduces differences because people simply make errors.* It is human to err even in what would appear to be a simple task; teachers are fallible. This leads to the next point.

4. *In education even measurement requires analysis and interpretation.* This point may surprise you somewhat. Yes, *measurement, as well as evaluation, requires you to analyze and interpret matters.* Things are not absolute; not black and white. In the spelling test, this point arises when people have trouble reading Janice Henry's handwriting. Is a word wrong in a spelling test if the handwriting is not neat? If an "i" is not dotted? If a "t" is not crossed?

If you wish to demonstrate this point further, use the Arithmetic Test Item with your group as given in the section "Suggestions and Comments." Present the item *during the debriefing* when dealing with the topic of measuring. Ask the group to *score* it on a scale from zero to ten. No doubt the participants in your group will differ on the score—that is, the amount of credit—to give this student. I generally receive a range of zero to eight when I use this arithmetic item with educators. Obviously, some people consider only accuracy, asking "Is the answer correct or not?" Other people consider effort. Still others consider the thinking processes used. In short, the item calls for analysis and interpretation in order to score it on a scale from zero to ten.

If measurement in such areas as spelling and arithmetic requires you to interpret the activity in some way, then all the more so is interpretation required in such subject matter areas as English, social studies, art, music, home economics, and health. Furthermore, interpretation in measurement is not limited to measurement of students in school subjects. Measurement of teacher behavior also requires the supervisor to interpret since in only rare instances are there absolutely right and wrong ways to measure. The supervisor must interpret the teaching context and the behavior even when "objectively describing" teacher talk with students. In short, 100 percent objectivity is not always possible. Rather, the supervisor and the teacher strive toward objectivity in measuring, which provides the basis for subsequent evaluation.

5. *An evaluative grade or comment is the result of considering many variables.* When the teacher gives the student a grade of A for a test or A for a course grade, the teacher must consider and weigh many variables. Similarly, when the supervisor recommends a teacher for merit-pay increment, the supervisor weighs a complex set of variables. Seldom, if ever, does a person evaluate the performance of another human being and consider only a single factor in reaching the decision given. Regarding the spelling test, people want to know the purpose of the test, Janice's general ability level, the criteria that are appropriate, and the performance of Janice's peers on the same test. To label Janice as a below-average (D) or above average (B) student knowing only that she spelled thirty-seven out of fifty-four words correctly and not knowing more about Janice, or the test, or the other students, or the criteria requires an act of great nerve. Similarly, to evaluate a teacher without much data and clear criteria is an audacious act because evaluation to be meaningful requires consideration of a cluster of variables bearing on the situation.

6. *It is difficult to score and grade a test or activity designed by someone else.* Every teacher-made test is designed in light of the teacher's purposes, the teacher's expectations of the students, the interaction which has occurred between the teacher and the students, and the criteria for success which the teacher has in mind. The test which the teacher gives to his students reflects these matters—the purpose, the expectations, the previous interaction, and the criteria. That is to say, *the test reflects the teacher, suggesting to all what the teacher considers important* in regard to each of these areas. Because of this it is difficult for one teacher to score and grade a test designed by another teacher. The second teacher simply is not party to the context within which the test was designed and probably cannot score or grade the test as intended.

For example, in The Spelling Test it is impossible to be sure about three words as you score it without the scoring key. These three are homonyms, sounding like other words but having a different spelling. They are: No. 12, dessert (desert); No. 45, seize (seas); and No. 50, they're (there, their). Unless you know the context and the design of Janice Henry's teacher, it is impossible to score these three words for sure though you may have a good idea about which words were intended. The context is all important regarding these three words.

Similarly, it is difficult for one supervisor to observe and evaluate a teacher who has had a series of interactions with another supervisor in which the purposes of teaching and supervision have been agreed upon, mutual goals have been set, and evaluative criteria have been clarified. A second supervisor entering the scene must spend some time learning the context and becoming party to the decisions reached. During this "orientation" period the second supervisor seeks to develop trust with the teacher because it is necessary to the supervisory relationship.

7. *Some evaluative standards are almost dogma now but deserve our close reconsideration.* Perhaps the most commonly accepted set of standards, with some minor modification, is the one which says that in terms of percentage and points scored: 100–90 merits an A; 80–89, a B; 70–79, a C; 60–69, a D; and below 60 an F or failure. I do not know the origin of this widely accepted set of standards, but it is clear that the ten-point ranges for each letter grade is a convenient but artificial, arbitrary, and restrictive way to convert test points to a letter grade. This set of standards based on the decimal system has achieved a status of being near dogma.

Nevertheless, we need to examine this set of standards that tradition gives to us. We need to ask such questions as: Should the distance between a C and a B be the same as between a B and an A? On what firm rational basis do we accept that a score of 90 to 100 percent correct merits an A? What modifications should be made to account for an easy test? What modifications should be made to account for a hard test? What alternative set of standards can we establish?

8. *Evaluation is necessary in education and consists of several components— measurement, analysis and interpretation, criteria (standards), and valuing.* Evaluation is necessary for students *and* for teachers. It is necessary not only because the law— whether it be state or local school board— requires us to evaluate. It is necessary because people do want to know how well they are doing. Many times people do not need an external evaluation of their performance but only a description of it to serve them as feedback. Then they proceed to evaluate themselves. That is, they determine on their own how well they are doing either by their own standards or an external set. Sometimes, however, people do seek an external evaluation. In any case, evaluation is present and necessary.

Evaluation consists of four distinct components. These components are (1) *measurement or description*; (2) *analysis and interpretation* of the data obtained; (3) *criteria or standards* that indicate what a "good" or "bad" performance are like; and (4) *valuing*, that is, placing a value on the performance by using such words as "excellent," "superior," "poor," and "fair." The valuing process requires us to match the analyzed and interpreted data against the criteria. The outcome is a value judgment. Often we do not express our final results in words but rather we *use symbols* to represent the value, such as A, B, C, D, and F or *, **, ***, and ****—a system often used to rate movies and restaurants. Not everyone proceeds in the same sequence. While some people begin with criteria and then move on to measurement, others begin with measurement and then develop their criteria. But whatever the sequence used we all get involved in the four components when we evaluate in education—whether as a teacher or as a supervisor.

9. *Measurement by the group is more accurate than measurement by the individual while valuing by the group is more complex and harder than valuing by the individual.* Members of the group are able to aid each other in measuring, one person correcting another's errors so that the net result is the elimination or at least reduction of error in measuring the performance under observation. As shown in Row G of Figure 8-4, each of the six small groups scored the test correctly. In each group there was at least one person who scored the test incorrectly. Nevertheless, that person did not prevail in determining the group score and the group scoring did not take much time.

On the other hand, assigning a value to the performance under observation requires considerable time because of the range of criteria used and the need to clarify the criteria in order to arrive at a common grade. The assigning of a grade is a more complex issue than measuring and involves interpreting the data and clarifying the criteria to be used by the group. The give and take of the grading process is quite different and takes longer than the give and take of the measuring process.

SUGGESTIONS AND COMMENTS

1.   Read through the entire activity, especially "Points Raised by Activity." This will help you to determine the direction in which you will guide the debriefing discussion. You can talk with teachers about the evaluation processes they use with regard to their students in their separate classes. Or, you can guide the discussion to be about evaluation of teachers. That is, you can discuss the implications of this "simple" spelling test for the "complex" situation of evaluating a student's or teacher's performance. The points raised by this activity will be rich enough to allow you to go either way or even both ways.

2. As you discuss the problems involved in measuring, you may find it helpful to present a simple Arithmetic Test Item.* (See Points Raised, No. 4.) The item is: If three apples cost 13 cents, how much will seven apples cost? Show your work.

$$
\begin{array}{r}
4.56 \\
3\overline{)13.00} \\
12 \\
\overline{1.0} \\
\underline{8} \\
20
\end{array}
\qquad
\begin{array}{r}
4.56 \\
\times \quad 7 \\
\hline
31.92
\end{array}
$$

Answer: *31.92*

*Used with permission of Ben M. Harris.

Ask each participant to give credit for this response on a scale of zero to ten. This is the first of ten arithmetic test items on a test for sixth graders, each item to be worth a maximum of ten points.

You can use this test item to enrich your discussion of the issues involved in the measuring component of evaluation. By using this item, you can easily talk about evaluation in subject areas other than spelling and then expand further to other subject areas. If you plan to use this, you may wish to have a separate handout sheet ready for distribution to each person. If a separate sheet is not available, you can quickly put the item on the chalkboard or overhead projection sheet.

3. If you are *very* pressed for time and wish to raise the topic of evaluation with a small number of participants who can then work together in the debriefing, you may be able to eliminate Step 8 of the "Procedure." This is not recommended, however, because this small-group step (Step 8) provides an excellent opportunity to engage in intimate, beneficial discussions on interpreting data and assigning grades. It also permits you to discuss accuracy of measurement in groups and possibly to apply the guidelines from Winter Crash Survival (see Chapter 7). If you do not request the use of the consensus approach for decision making, you have an excellent springboard to discuss the different processes that the various groups employed in reaching their decision on grades.

4. You can conduct this entire activity in about seventy-five minutes. If you have more time, you can go slowly, especially in Step 8 and Step 9 regarding the meaning of the activity for both teaching and supervision. If you must speed up, you can skip the Arithmetic Test Item and possibly the group decision step, or you can limit the time allotted to group deciding. Whatever you decide, leave at least thirty minutes for debriefing and moving forward, Steps 9 and 10. These steps are most important since they allow you to relate this activity to your particular situation.

5. If you are a principal, for example, and do not feel comfortable leading this activity with your faculty, by all means ask someone else to lead it. Perhaps the school's or district's research and evaluation expert will lead this activity for you. You can be a participant or observer, as you see fit.

APPLICATIONS

The Spelling Test touches directly on every educator's life. We are all involved in the components of evaluation daily. Teachers use tests often to diagnose their students' progress, to help in evaluating their students' achievement, and to motivate their students. Whatever the reason for testing the students, the teachers must measure, analyze and interpret data, and consider the criteria they will use when they assign a valuative grade or write an evaluative report based on the tests they have given. At the same time, the supervisors who must make recommendations about tenure, renewing contracts, and merit-pay increments are involved in the evaluation of the teachers, or at least the observation (description), analysis and interpretation of data, and criteria components of evaluation. Therefore, it is important to apply the ideas raised in the activity session to the ongoing life of the faculty; it is important to build on the activity.

SPECIAL MEMO

As with the other structured activities, one simple way to start a follow-up on The Spelling Test activity is to send a memo to each person reminding the faculty of several key points raised and the suggestions made for future use. Figure 8-5 offers an easy form to use as a quick and effective method for informing your faculty about your perspective on the training session. Your selection of quotable quotes and points raised will serve to let people know how you feel about the session.

Figure 8-6 shows a completed form. Here Jim Groshen, an elementary school principal, uses three quotations and three concepts to show that the concern with evaluation is strong. Furthermore, it is clear from the bottom section that he is serious about rethinking the grading system used in his school. He has chosen to devote an entire faculty meeting to the topic and to begin by discussing a position paper to be drawn up by a faculty member. In this way, the faculty will come prepared to discuss the topic while the experiences of the training session are fresh in their minds.

SUPERVISION

When you meet with your faculty members individually, you have an excellent opportunity to pursue the topic of evaluation further. You can begin, for example, by working with the teacher in terms of the evaluation system used by the teacher in regard to his students. You can examine with him how he measures student progress—frequency, instruments, and results. You can also discuss the criteria he uses in giving grades. Talking about evaluation of students will provide a fairly easy, smooth way to pursue the topic of evaluation in supervision later.

As you confer with your faculty about supervision, you can readily refer to The Spelling Test activity to highlight the various components of evaluation. By referring to

TO: _____

FROM: _____

RE: Follow-up from The Spelling Test

Led by _____ on _____, 19____

1. Quotable quotes from the session:

    A.

    B.

    C.

2. Key points raised:

    A.

    B.

    C.

3. Decisions to follow through for implementation:

FIGURE 8-5. Follow-up memo for The Spelling Test (blank).

TO: <u>Faculty</u>

FROM: <u>Jim Groshen</u>

RE: Follow-up from The Spelling Test

　　　Led by <u>me</u>　　　　　　　　　on <u>March 19</u> , 19<u>XX</u>

1. Quotable quotes from the session:

   A. "I pity the substitutes who must administer one of my tests; I struggle with them myself."

   B. "We need to rethink our grading system."

   C. "Sure we all knew that evaluation is subjective but we weren't yet ready to accept the idea that measurement is interpretive, too."

2. Key points raised:

   A. Measuring is tough but grading is tougher still.

   B. The context of an evaluation is all important.

   C. Without clear criteria known to all we'll never have a school-wide policy on evaluation.

3. Decisions to follow through for implementation:
   Our next meeting will be devoted to standardizing our grading system. Judy has volunteered to present a proposal to us. She'll distribute a copy to everyone before the meeting. Please read it carefully before we begin so we can start the discussion of it promptly at 3 p.m. after a brief comment by Judy.

FIGURE 8-6. Follow-up memo for The Spelling Test (filled in).

the training session and any conferences about student evaluation, you have available to you parallel situations to help clarify the issues and problems you yourself face with your faculty. You can discuss the issue of potential error when you describe a teacher's performance during an observational visit, the issue of comparative performances—the teacher compared to others as mentioned in the research literature and/or as you have observed in your experience as an educator—and the issue of criteria of effectiveness.

FACULTY MEETINGS OR COMMITTEES

Since evaluation is a persistent issue in education, you can ask the faculty to reconsider the evaluation system being used in your school in regard to the four components—measurement, analysis and interpretation, criteria, and valuing. You can ask teachers to make presentations at a meeting, either in terms of what they do, how to improve personally in one aspect of evaluation, or how to alter the system on a school-wide basis. You can form a task force to draw up a proposal for faculty consideration or for submission eventually to the board of education for its approval. The important thing is to use The Spelling Test activity as a springboard to open up the topic for discussion of issues that directly affect your faculty.

CONCLUDING WORDS

Evaluation is a complex persistent issue which demands our continued attention because it vitally affects the daily lives of most people in our school. This is true whether we are concerned primarily with students who take hundreds of tests during their school days and are evaluated formally on report cards several times a year or whether we are concerned primarily with teachers who are dependent on positive evaluations for their livelihood. The components of the evaluation process and the issues they raise are essentially the same in either case and for this reason the points raised when discussing Janice Henry's spelling test apply to teaching as well as supervision.

We need to look closely at this structured activity, The Spelling Test, because the insights we have regarding it can shed light on the evaluations we do in teaching and supervision. We need to be alert to measurement error, unclear criteria, and interpretation of data so that when we involve ourselves in evaluation of someone else's performance we can do so fairly, humanely, cautiously, and wisely. When we are alert to the issues persisting in the evaluation process, we can take steps to avoid problems and to improve our skill as well as our judgment. The Spelling Test activity is useful in sensitizing us to these matters and is therefore beneficial to educators.

CHAPTER 8 ENDNOTE

1.   B. HARRIS, W. BESSENT, and K. MCINTYRE, "A Spelling Test," *In-Service Education* (Englewood Cliffs, N.J.: Prentice-Hall, Inc., 1969), 66. (Modifications used with the permission of the authors.)

INDEX

V

Videotape recording, 52
Voting
    alternatives to majority vote, 24–25
    consensus as an alternative to, 26
    delegation as an alternative to, 25
    importance of, 5–6
    reasons against, 24
    reasons for, 22, 24

W

Winter Crash Survival activity
    applications of, 124, 130
    conclusions regarding, 130
    materials needed for, 111
    number of participants for, 111
    overview of, 110–11
    points raised by, 119, 121–23
    procedure for, 111, 114, 117, 119
    suggestions and comments regarding,
        123